A Full-Length Play:

Anna Nicole: Blonde Glory

And

Three Short Absurdist Plays

by Grace Cavalieri

Copyright © 2023 by Grace Cavalieri

Forest Woods Media Productions

All rights reserved. No part of this book can be reproduced, or transmitted in any form or by any means, electronic or mechanical, including photocopying, recording, or by any information storage and retrieval system without requesting permission and giving credit to the author.

Library of Congress Control Number: 2023908000
ISBN 978-0-938572-69-5

Anna Nicole Painting by Holly Picano
Book design and cover graphics by Henry Crawford

Table of Contents

Foreword i

Sunshine Tiki Villas 1

Harvest Kitchen 23

Cuffed Frays 31

Anna Nicole: Blonde Glory 59

About the Author 141

Foreword

A Full-Length Play: "Anna Nicole: Blonde Glory"
And
Three Short Absurdist Plays
By Grace Cavalieri

Why am I committing these plays to print now? Well, simply because they never got a fair share of the audiences they deserved; and are now enjoying small Salon Readings, keeping them alive. "Anna Nicole: Blonde Glory" was in development for five years, with several successful readings in Maryland and New York City. It was guided to production by Director Shela Xoregos. The play opened at The Theater for The New City, (NYC) in October 2012. There was a marvelous opening night and then Sandy the Hurricane hit the city, filling the subways with water, and closing Broadway and off-Broadway for weeks. When calm was restored, our show was closed, since it was mounted as a three- week showcase production, and all actors were off to other jobs. Rose Solari portrayed "Anna" at The Bethesda Writers' Center in its initial reading.

"ANNA NICOLE: BLONDE GLORY: a poignant and witty play by Grace Cavalieri, award-winning poet and playwright. An imagined panorama of Anna Nicole Smith's life. The cast of six stars Mary Riley as Anna Nicole-a portrayal seemingly channelled from the model herself. Composer Jon Tomlinson creates a sound score and a cheer-leading production number for Anna to sing and dance. Costumes: Rayneese Primrose; lighting: Don Cate; Shela Xoregos directs." New York Theatre News.

"Cuffed Frays" won a state-wide playwriting contest in West Virginia 2001, was produced for radio, but deserved a live viewing. The play was revived in a salon reading, 2022, with Phyllis Culham and Grace Cavalieri performing the roles of Chester and Jo.
Also in 2022, to an invited audience, "Sunshine Tiki Villas" premiered with actors Nancy Buchenauer, Nancy Zimmerman, and Phyllis Culham, portraying Veronica, Coco, and Muriel.

"Harvest Kitchen" was originally written as a short story in 1976. At that time the piece won the Pen Syndicated Fiction Award, judged by Grace Palin. After this, 'Harvest Kitchen" was converted to a short two -character play. Although previously produced for radio, the "live" Reading was premiered by Janice Booth (Fran) and Jackie Graves (Margaret) in 2022, as part of the Annapolis Maryland Salon Series.

These three short plays, which had such small lives, still endure and now are made permanent so their characters, who deserved more, can flourish a little longer. Additionally, Anna Nicole Smith, who was so devalued in her own life, is vindicated in this fiction and is therefore worth saving in print.

Grace Cavalieri
Annapolis, MD
2023

Sunshine Tiki Villas

Sunshine Tiki Villas

by Grace Cavalieri

***

Characters: Coco, an older woman
              Muriel, an older woman
              Veronica, an older woman

Place: A bungalow in the Tiki Villas.
Time: The Present

Coco   I don't know what I'm doing here.

Muriel You're with me.

Coco   I'm always with you.

Muriel Women live longer.

Coco   Than what?

Muriel Than other people.

Coco   Oh.

Muriel When we take care of each other.

Coco   You're not doing a very good job.

Muriel You're not the easiest, what with your plant-based foods.

Coco   Is the world just a projection of us, Muriel?

Muriel	I'd hate to think the world smelled like chicken soup and Lysol.
Coco	And urine.
Muriel	And urine.
Coco	That's why we are staying here at the Villas. It's so cheerful.
Muriel	Now why are you crying?
Coco	I'm crying because...
Muriel	(*Warning*) We've talked about this, Coco.
Coco	Because...
Muriel	We made a bargain not to give in. We have a show of strength to put on here at The Villas.
Coco	O.K. I'm crying because I'm happy.
Muriel	That's better. What shall we do today?
Coco	We could get started on this (*Gets shoebox from table.*)
Muriel	On what?
Coco	Sorting through these words in the shoebox. Memorizing them.

Muriel All the words people lose.

Coco Yesterday I tripped on the… on the… and couldn't remember the word for sidewalk. So I wrote it down and when it happens again I'll just check in here (indicates box.)

Muriel The shoebox is getting full.

Coco Well people need choices.

Muriel I tripped on the…

Coco I'd wait 30 seconds, it's only fair…. We may recall.

Muriel I tripped on (picks out word from shoebox) **FLORIDA.**

Coco Oh yes. Many proper nouns saved here. They're the first to go.

Muriel Tripped on *Florida*.

Coco It may help people who come to visit us.

Muriel Everyone loses words.

Coco Everyone loses everything that ever lived.

Muriel Stop it Coco.

Coco I'm happy about it (*crying*). This is how I look when I'm happy.

(*Doorbell*)

Coco	I'll get it. (*Enter Veronica with suitcase*) (*Coco whispers*) You weren't to come downstairs yet (*looks at watch*) until next month.
Veronica	There's no heat up there. (*Veronica kisses her on the mouth*).
Coco	(*Brushes her away*) I don't care – this is not our plan.
Muriel	(*Enter Muriel*) Who is this?
Coco	Veronica, I'd like you to meet Muriel. Muriel, Veronica
Veronica	How do you do.
Coco	I was going to explain later, Veronica, but Muriel and I got into somewhat of a spat … and this is a surprise to me as well….
Veronica	Where do I put this? (*Sets down suitcase*)
Muriel	What do you mean?
Veronica	Where do I stash my clothes? The rest are coming.
Muriel	Well certainly not here! Coco?
Veronica	Okay okay. Let's all sit down. May I?

Muriel	I don't want to sit down.
Coco	Well I think you need to, Muriel. Veronica has come to stay.
Muriel	Stay.
Coco	With us.
Muriel	You and me. Where?
Coco	She can't live upstairs forever.
Muriel	Upstairs!
Coco	She's been here weeks already.
Muriel	Upstairs... our villa? And I didn't know it? How could this be? What does this mean. Coco!
Veronica	She didn't know how to break it to you.
Muriel	I guess not.
Coco	I let her.
Muriel	This isn't your villa only.
Coco	I know I know I did it anyway.
Muriel	You didn't care what I thought? Felt? This is my home too.
Coco	There's a part of me that does things like this.

Veronica	Alien love.
Muriel	Upstairs in our house? *(to Veronica)* Why?
Veronica	I like people.
Muriel	Yes?
Veronica	And I like being alone.
Muriel	So?
Veronica	But I don't like those two things at one time.
Muriel	How does that explain my house.
Veronica	I could be alone upstairs.
Muriel	That's true.
Veronica	And you said you didn't even know I was there so what's the fuss.
Muriel	That's because we've always had squirrels or raccoons.
Veronica	Well I would hear you down here-your coffee cups in the morning. The spoons on the table top ... it was so quiet and I felt part of it. Family! But I didn't have to face you to say Good Morning. I hate that.
Muriel	Well I'll be damned.

Coco	Maybe I should explain she didn't have a place to stay and there's our empty attic and it has a toilet, when Aunt Edna lived here.
Veronica	The sound was nice and dry for my violin.
Muriel	You played a violin in my attic?
Veronica	When you went off to the dining hall or to your crafts and bazaars.
Muriel	(*to Coco*) You You You...
Coco	You always take the conventional view. That's what's the matter with you. At painting class on Thursdays, everything is brown with you...never a smidgen of red.
Muriel	Someone lives upstairs in my attic without my knowing it-how long?
Veronica	Oh, six months or better. The palm tree outside was first put in, and now look at the size.
Muriel	They are fake palms.
Coco	One of the advantages here. Reason we bought here, remember Muriel.
Muriel	Quiet Coco. (*To Veronica*) You played a violin for 6 months up there?

Veronica	Everyday. Oh not very well I'm afraid.
Muriel	Coco this is against the law!
Coco	What law? I'm like your sister.
Muriel	Breaking and entering.
Coco	I had a key.
Muriel	The law of civility.
Veronica	She didn't hurt anyone. You didn't even know I was here. What's uncivil about that?
Coco	What's the difference. Let her be. What harm can it do?
Veronica	I can give you money. You want money?
Muriel	I don't think that's the principle at stake here.
Veronica	I can play the violin for you (*Brings violin out of suitcase*)
Muriel	Sit down both of you. I want you to understand. I am a woman. Not a man. If I want someone to like me I do not need to use money.
Coco	That's for sure. She's very cheap.
Veronica	So you don't want my money then?

Coco	She didn't say that.
Muriel	I'm trying to tell you-you are corrupting my life here. You are making up rules I don't believe in.
Coco	No one suffered here, Muriel. No one suffered but Veronica. You were perfectly happy the whole time so what harm was done?
Veronica	I couldn't even use the front entrance. Down the back steps. Always up and down the steps. And they don't even have backs on the steps. You can see the sky between. Very unsettling. Are you sure you don't want to hear a little sonata?
Coco	Can't I keep her Muriel? She won't eat much. Please? Oh please.
Muriel	I am not a mean person. I'm just too old to start again.
Coco	There are no extra villas at all, Muriel. We checked.
Muriel	I can't learn another person's habits, to tell her my allergies, to explain why I stay in bed when it rains; you have to tell someone everything about yourself all over again. I'm too old to start again. I'm too tired for anything new.
Veronica	Ladies, ladies, let us come to terms. May I speak frankly?

Muriel   Please.

Veronica   Let us look at this a different way. *(She pushes each person to a different place in the room, setting them there)* There now we have a fresh view of each other. I came here because I had no place to go.

Muriel   That is not my problem.

Veronica   Wait listen. Neither of you has any place to go. No one has a place to go. No one cares if you live. No one is waiting on the porch for you, either of you. You've outlived your use. The world is small if you don't have wings…You are sitting here in your # 12 Villa with nowhere to go. That's why I'm here.

Muriel   How's that?

Veronica   At least I do something. I came here. I went somewhere. You two never had the guts to even do that.

Muriel   I think you're really crazy.

Veronica   You two are close, yes? And have been together a long time since you were young.

Coco   Oh yes through the anus of time.

Muriel   I think the word is anals.

Veronica	I think the word is annals.
Coco	Whichever - we've been friends.
Veronica	Covenants. Don't each one of you want to make a change before you die? That's why I went upstairs. I was tired of being afraid.
Muriel	What does this have to do with invading my house?
Veronica	I was invited by Coco. When was the last thing you did something new.
Coco	Everything passes, Muriel. It could be quite natural for Veronica to do things and live here with us.
Muriel	It's about our cells. People swap cells. Back and forth if they're together. I'm careful about that! (*Storms off.*)
Coco	(*takes Veronicq aside*) Should we tell her about our plans?
Veronica	Which ones?
Coco	You know, fixing the house up for our music students.
Veronica	Not yet. She seems unstable.
Coco	That's true I'll leave you two alone for a few minutes. Try to make up to her. Flatter her.

	Think of something. Ask her about life. Tell her a story, a tragic one; tell her your mother died. Get close. I'll get the tea (*Exit Coco.*)
Muriel	(*Enters ... to Veronica*) I thought Coco would never leave. Did you? (*She kisses Veronica on the lips*)
Veronica	There for a moment I thought she was suspicious as if she knew something.
Muriel	What could she know. She's stupid.
Veronica	Well, I thought I should have looked guiltier.
Muriel	How do we get rid of her so we can fix up the house for our music students.
Veronica	Is this going to backfire on us?
Muriel	Give it time. I'll keep up the hostility and you keep being impervious and we'll see where it takes us.
Veronica	'Where it takes us' is not a plan.
Muriel	We could surprise her with the truth and watch her explode.
Veronica	She's your only living friend and in your living trust. I am not cutting that ribbon.
Muriel	She's not getting anything anyway.

(Coco enters)

Veronica	(*To Muriel, as if begging*) I have nothing. I spent a life in service to my family.
Muriel	This is not a welfare stop.
Veronica	By the looks of you two I can see I waited too long to come here.
Muriel	Especially since you weren't invited in the first place.
Coco	You could be fresh air. We left our husbands and look at us now.
Muriel	They died, Coco.
Coco	We still left them afterwards. And now I have Muriel.
Muriel	And I have Coco. It's been a less than positive experience.
Veronica	The question at hand is what do we do now?
Coco and Muriel	Do?
Muriel	How are we going to get out of this mess?
Coco	We're not in a mess. We're three lonely people who live together.

Muriel	No I live here. You joined me and Veronica is a carpet bagger.
Veronica	I'd go back if I could I swear but I feel I'm meant to be here.
Muriel	Go back where.
Veronica	To memory ... to the past ... but when I get there no one's home.
Muriel	Poor Veronica. Life has passed you by too. I know I myself never learned chess.
Coco	Or Russian.
Muriel	And now there's computer animation. It's always something.
Veronica	I'll go to the attic and practice. I always played on Tuesday when you were both away.
Coco	Knitting is on Tuesday at noon.
Muriel	(*To Veronica*) What are you practicing music for?
Veronica	Whatever event will show up. Real or imagined.
Muriel	If life is an illusion, maybe we should just sit it out to the end.

Coco	You know what I wish. That when you turn the TV on people were really there.
Veronica	It's on tape.
Muriel	So sad.
Veronica	That's why I play, I'll play for you.
Coco	Someday later, Veronica.
Muriel	When we feel better.
Veronica	My husband was always looking for an escape route when I played. Shifted his eyes. They went from side to side.
Muriel	A less than positive sign, yes.
Veronica	What of yours?
Muriel	I scarcely remember him.
Veronica	And you Coco?
Coco	It's shameless what a person can feel. I'd rather not say.
Muriel	There's so much besides the world of marriage.
Veronica	That's why the violin is better. Music.
Coco	And Muriel's husband was unfaithful.

Muriel	Oh I already forgot who we were talking about.
Coco	Feelings.
Veronica	There are no feelings in the afterlife you know.
Coco	What has that got to do with anything, dear.
Muriel	Well it is something to look forward to.
Coco	Everything changes.
Muriel	Oh yes. The Orient is called Asia now. Everything changes.
Coco	Veronica, clear something up for me. What do you want?
Veronica	Autonomy, but with people.
Muriel	And you Coco?
Coco	This time of day? Dinner.
Muriel	This puts me in an awkward place. It always impinges on me, I can't provide either of you what you want. So I am the one burdened it seems.
Veronica	You are both a mess of broken dreams, and so ending up like this will not do. The end of your life is most important because that is the way

	you'll begin your *next* life...You want to be failures next time too?
Coco	I want to wear mesh stockings.
Muriel	I wanted to be in the circus once.
Veronica	Aha.
Muriel	And I was so young but I joined up. I had never done anything and I was thinner then. I wanted to be loved but I was so shy.
Coco	I became a nun.
Veronica	Yes if you can believe in God you can believe in anything. I understand that.
Coco	I thought it would help but I was lousy at that too.
Muriel	So she became a lesbian.
Coco	Muriel.
Muriel	Just for a year.
Veronica	She was lousy at that too trust me (dead silence.)
Muriel	Veronica!
Coco	Muriel!

Coco (*To Muriel*) But you did marry. I knew him, your ex.

Muriel Adultery

Veronica You committed adultery?

Coco Muriel hardly committed marriage. I knew him well, her ex.

Muriel Ok. Out with it Coco! You forgot the time I walked in and caught you sitting on the couch. He had his head in your lap? And you were entirely naked. Entirely.

Veronica Naked usually assumes entirely, dear.

Coco And what did he say!

Muriel He said he hadn't noticed.

Coco You could have given him the benefit of the doubt.

Veronica You believed him?

Muriel Of course not. I told him to get up and get dressed also.

Coco Muriel makes so much of everything.

Muriel Oh, he was dapper alright.

Coco	And every time Muriel wasn't looking, he held my hand up to his cheek and kissed the palm of my hand.
Muriel	An outrage.
Coco	It's shameless what a person can feel and do.
Muriel	This is all too much. (*Sits dizzily*) I am just on the verge of…of…of…I am on the verge of …

(Coco rushes to her with shoebox)

Coco:	Here. Here Muriel. (Sits by Muriel and takes her hand)
Muriel	(Muriel picks a word)… of cosmetology.
Veronica	Yes. Aren't we all. Aren't we all. (*Sits by Coco and takes her hand and kisses the palm.*)

(Door bell rings. Veronica jumps up, grabs her suitcase and violin case.)

Veronica:	That's for me. I must be going. I have some others to tend to. Remember, do not be afraid! Take the plunge into whatever you fear.

(Exit)

Coco
and Muriel   Afraid of what?

(They look at each other and dump the box, scrambling through the papers as play ends looking perplexed at each other)

THE END

Harvest Kitchen

Harvest Kitchen

by Grace Cavalieri

***

Characters: Fran, a middle aged women
Margaret, a middle aged woman

Scene: A table and two chairs

Fran   You've been coming here for 10 years for lunch.

Margaret   Yes. But I missed that time you went to Florida.

Fran   Yes. Sometimes you missed.

Margaret   And the hurricane. When the creek was high I didn't come.

Fran   That's not to the point and you know it.

Margaret   What is the point? I want it for the record. Straight.

Fran   You never so much as said – in ten years' time – you liked the cake.

Margaret   Ok so this is good cake.

Fran   Don't be smart. This is soup.

Margaret	What's in a name. Appreciation is what you want. It's what you'll get.
Fran	You never say "Frances, you did a good job. You always say "This is a good job. Like it was the job who did good. Like you said "This is good cake."
Margaret	Soup.
Fran	Yes? Yes?
Margaret	Maybe I think it's a good job in spite of you doing it…or maybe I don't like it and don't want to make you feel responsible, so I lie and say it's a good job or "a good meal."
Fran	No.
Margaret	No?
Fran	No. It doesn't work out. No.
Margaret	How come, Mrs. Freud-Herself?
Fran	I am not appreciated.
Margaret	Prove it.
Fran	When I wear a dress you say "That's a nice dress." You never once say "You look nice" and

	when I got a haircut, you said "He gave you a good haircut."
Margaret	You think you could do better yourself? Including the back of the hair where you can't see?
Fran	You act like I'm not here.
Margaret	How could this be? We got soup here to prove you're here. How could you feel invisible?
Fran	I want you to know something. I want you to know I will not be home on next Tuesday. Not on Tuesday next week.
Margaret	Where will I go?
Fran	So you come here because you have nothing whatsoever to do with your Tuesdays. Is that what you're saying to me?
Margaret	Not especially. If I was used to Thursday, that'd be the feeling I have about not coming on next Thursday.
Fran	This will hurt. But – if you visited next Thursday – I wouldn't be home next Thursday. So there. Get the message – from me to you?
Margaret	All this fuss.
Fran	All this fuss indeed.

Margaret Just because I didn't compliment this rotten food. Made from leftovers, I'm sure of it. And hard to eat next to this plant of yours the cat visits occasionally.

Fran Are you going to bring poor Peter into this conversation about us? Isn't that a nice smoke screen though.

Margaret Forget the animal. He's scroungy looking to boot. We're talking about leftovers you overrate by calling them lunch." And I saw you, by the way, drop a piece of meat on the floor and dust it off to serve.

Fran Why have you waited ten years to insult me?

Margaret I got back. Fed the meat to Peter, I did. Right in front of you, pretending I was patting his head.

Fran Vengeful. That's what you are.

Margaret Revenge is the only way of getting back if you're a guest. What could a guest do? Make a fuss?

Fran Oh aren't you the mannerly one, now.

Margaret Well that's it for us I guess.

Fran After ten years of friendship.

Margaret	Things change, I saw that on TV, never the same program.
Fran	I'll just get my calendar then.

(Pause)

Margaret	Yes. It looks like next week it will be Wednesday.
Fran	I can do Wednesday, but I hope things can return to normal.
Margaret	If some people can stop complaining.
Fran	See you Wednesday.
Margaret	Yes, but don't always depend on Wednesdays. I can only take so much.

THE END

Cuffed Frays

Cuffed Frays

by Grace Cavalieri

***

Characters: Jo, a middle aged woman
Chester, her husband
Millie, a slightly younger woman
Reverend, parish priest, mature

(We hear cat's meowing and Jo's voice coming in close, as if from across the room) (meowing stops)

Jo   The sudden coolness in here around the house. It has to do with a lack of greenery you never understood *(close) (Sounds of sitting)* When you had your stroke and fell out your chair, didn't I catch you? And after thinking, somehow, it was my fault. That's what a person gets for doing a good deed for a friend.

Chester   Husband.

Jo   Well, I was thinking friend was more to the way of saying something better than husband. Didn't I catch you? Well then, why do I think it was my fault? I get nervous every time you sit.

Chester   I can't keep standing.

Jo   That's not the point at all.

Chester   I think it's jealousy on your part, Jo, your way of helping me. Like when I fell out. I don't

	connect it all but I think somehow you're jealous that I had something first for a change.
Jo	Now I know your artery's closed down on you all the way to talk like that.
Chester	I never heard you give a compliment that wasn't in jealousy. It's your failing. Your biggest failing – besides being vicious the way you are.
Jo	Come on old man. Because you're lonely and for no other reason you talk like that. When I go to the grocer's you get lonely and I have to pay my way when I get back – alright, I'm doing it right now, aren't I, taking your complaints in my stride, in my uncomplicated way.
Chester	They don't call it "grocer's" anymore, and they haven't for years. They haven't since, maybe World War II.
Jo	A grocer's a grocer. You try to sidetrack me with information, you do. Logistics. You're the one with all the facts just when I'm hot to the heat of the matter like that. The grocer.
Chester	Or that next war after. They don't name them now. Nothing has a name on it. You have to remember the whole bloody globe and places who weren't there when you were a child, in the first place.

Jo	This loneliness of yours makes you accusatory to me. Like our own one-eyed cat there. If he's got mucous, he's seeing mice out of every corner, alright.
Chester	You were the one who wanted him for the streaks in his fur.
Jo	I admit it.
Chester	Well admit it then.
Jo	I do. I admit I loved the yellow, circular like it is.
Chester	You like to be different all the time. Always have liked that. Thank God you're out of the bloody costumes you used to wear down the street. Beads and lace. You looked like something out of Old Arsenic. Things have changed, Jo. And you with it, to the better. To the better. I'll admit that much.
Jo	Thank you.
Chester	Remember the farmer story from up in New Hampshire where...
Jo	Get on with it.
Chester	He said, "I've felt so much for you all these years..."

Jo	O.K. Come out with it. Don't make a career over everything you say.
Chester	"felt so much for you all these years, it's been all I could do to keep from telling you?"
Jo	I do. I do remember.
Chester	There's a message in it for you, from me.
Jo	And back to you.
Chester	Thanks, Jo, but that's your form of aggression, Josephine. There we have a perfect example.
Jo	Nothing's perfect, Chester.
Chester	Putting your emotions inside someone else the way you do – occupying their territory like that. Sitting in ownership on their brain – rocking on it like a seesaw. A perfect example here. We can see it. You telling me what I'm feeling.
Jo	I didn't say two words about how you're feeling. I'm getting us some hot water and sugar with a lemon slice in it at this very moment. That'll clear the air.
Chester	Acts as a cathartic. Jo, you turn my head like a faucet.

Jo	Hmm. A wedge of lemon will do you good. Suck it after it's been floating hot. It cleans the mouth – acid – kills germs.
Chester	Are you proposing I wipe myself with it too then?
Jo	No need to get huffy like you do. I'm serving you a lovely cup of tea – without the tea. It gets you agitated. No tea.
Chester	It's my agitation. I'm allowed. I'm the one has to live with it.
Jo	You? Up all night. Telling me I begrudge you your sleep… putting on earphones and making body sounds you think nobody else can hear. You can't hear your own self when you have wind and you think no one else in the universe can. Self-deception. There's a living proof, right there.
Chester	Am I really that much different than anyone else, Josephine? To hear you reading off my dimensions makes me feel like the first man on the moon.
Jo	You couldn't be the first man, Chester. Not the first.
Chester	No no – not the first. History's done that for us. But I'm speaking of how you make me feel. The intensity of how you make me feel – of trying to live up there, trying to grow

	something on the moon in the cold. That's just the way of saying how cut off I feel – even when you're in this very room.
Jo	Have your cup, Chester. Let the lemon float first.
Chester	It's as if you say I should straighten up. Straighten up. Straighten up or you won't love me. Straighten up or you won't hold my actions against me.
Jo	Jesus. You got a mouth on you, would have made a senator cry.
Chester	Can you direct your address a little more accurately to me, Jo. Am I really so different?
Jo	No no no no no Chester, you're not. You're not. Stir the bottom there. You're just very much more so than the others. You have a round brain or something. It's like a ball I could drop off.
Chester	I like your language today, Jo my love. You have a penchant today, Jo, and I must say the hot water's just tasty and hot. Just right. Delicious.
Jo	Hmm.
Chester	Flat language's the one thing I won't tolerate. "Round brain." Now that's nice.

Jo	Um.
Chester	You create an aura, you do, when you get on to it, Jo. You can hold your own with the best.
Jo	Dripping there.
Chester	Oh, sorry. Purity, intensity and unity, I always say.
Jo	Purity, intensity and unity. Sounds like a beer ad.
Chester	It's my saying, meaning, when you have this – I could tell you everything I think, you know.
Jo	Hm.
Chester	My fantasies
Jo	Um. Your fantasies now.
Chester	I once thought how it'd be if someone took a cigarette and held it right to that cat's one good eye.
Jo	*(Silence. Clears throat.)*
Chester	I often wondered if it'd make a sizzle – being that it's so moist if it'd smell like anything burning. Or if he'd have pain. You know, serious thoughts like that.

Jo	Chester, you are the world's longest tape recorder. I'd like to put some earphones on me.
Chester	What? What? *(laughs)* Stomach pain? *(laughs uproariously)*
Jo	You're a disgusting old man.
Chester	*(stops laughing.)*
Jo	People should never laugh at their own humor. That means it's really not funny at all. Perverse.
Chester	I wouldn't call me perverse if I were you.
Jo	Well you're not.
Chester	I didn't say I'd ever take a cigarette and do it. Why do you not separate what I say from what I am?
Jo	Blind cats indeed.
Chester	I wasn't half serious.
Jo	You know he matters to me.
Chester	Oh now, look at you getting glum. I know, he matters to me too.
Jo	Twelve years we've had him. That's as old as they get. He sleeps in the cellar, not even

	bothering you. One day he'll go down the steps and just not come up and that'll be that.
Chester	I wish to apologize for that – what I said. And him with one eye leaking and bleeding, hanging on so with the luster still in his round fur, well, fur's not round – the color in it, yes.
Jo	Logistics again, is it?
Chester	I care for him too. I do. I'm used to him from A to Z.
Jo	Hm.
Chester	Well now.
Jo	You're done.
Chester	And a fine cup it was.
Jo	Give it here. *(sounds of china)*
Chester	Delicious and sweet toward the bottom.
Jo	You want to dip the rind in the sugar?
Chester	I scraped it out with my finger and sucked it already.
Jo	Well, to each his own. Just that the tart and the sweet are good together – but it's my taste, not yours.

Chester	Yup. I'm going for a walk in the sun now.
Jo	This time of day?
Chester	So?
Jo	Naptime.
Chester	Can't we do something new?
Jo	Sure we can, but late afternoon – the light is weak – not warm for walking.
Chester	Naptime is sad. I wake – then I get depressed when it's late day. Then it's dinner by the stove. Then, night I'm up and down all night. So that's why I thought I'd walk.
Jo	I'm coming along.
Chester	Suit yourself.
Jo	I'm getting the sweater here. We'll carry a supper of sorts and sit down and have it together.
Chester	Where at?
Jo	Where you going for this walk?
Chester	Well I don't know. This is becoming special now, isn't it?

Jo   This one time, do you suppose the cat could come?

Chester   I could suppose all I want, Jo. Cats do not wish to accompany folks on their walks.

(The sound of "Victrola" music)

          No, Jo, you're not going through the dance with the cat now or I'll go outside and…

Jo   If you do – it'll be the <u>last</u> time you relieve yourself in my garden.

Chester   There's nothing I can do otherwise to get you to know I'm serious about my contentions.

Jo   Relieving yourself. Streaming the stone wall. No. It won't do.

(Cat meows)

Chester   He hates it when you pick up his front paw.

Jo   He loves it.

Chester   He's too old.

Jo   *(Winded)* He could always hop on his back feet.

Chester   He don't want to dance anymore.

Jo	*(Sound of sitting, plopping)* You do it. I'll watch.
Chester	I promise you this – the cat will know we're coming back even if you don't waltz with him.
Jo	How? How will he know?
Chester	Well he just will. You can't lose a cat. It's been often said.

(Door opening. Music off.)

Jo	It's been often said... it's been often said... I suppose that's to satisfy me, like when I point out your inferior traits (mimics him) "That may be true" like it's supposed to make everything acceptable.

(Door slams)

Chester	I'm inside.
Jo	*(Door opens)* I'm out.
Chester	No lunch then in the woods?
Jo	No. Not time for us now. The cat will be ready for his beef liver. We can't push everything together to the end.

(Door closes.)

Chester	I'm out.

Jo	I see.

(Sounds of walking on leaves.) (Steps approaching their own.)

Millie	Mr. Henry. Mr. Henry.

Jo	Millie, whatever…

Millie	I ran all the way.

Jo	For God's sake, I've never even seen you walk fast, what with your weight.

Millie	*(Breaks into sobs)* I cannot tell you what just happened.

Chester	Well don't then.

Jo	Chester!

Millie	*(Sobs)* I was strolling

Chester	*(Snorts)* I'm going, Jo.

Millie	With this man…

Chester	*(impatient throat noise)*

Millie	And he said…

Chester	I'm going over by the wall.

Millie	And he said the worst thing.

(walking) (sounds) (Chester walking off)

Millie	He said something I could never repeat in a million years.
Jo	*(Calls)* You do, Chester and it'll be the last time.

(Millie steps closer)

Chester	I'm just looking at the garden *(distant)*
Jo	You were out an hour ago looking.
Millie	He said something so awful, I can't … I can't.
Jo	Chester is incontinent and he knows it irritates me.

(Sounds of rummaging. Small items drop)

Jo	Whatever you are.
Millie	My pencil – a pencil. I'll… I'll write down what he said.
Jo	I'm sorry Millie, you're so upset but I'll be on my way if you are writing me a note. I have my limits.

(Walks away)

Millie	Mrs. Henry. *(paper rattling)* He said, "I *(sob)* "want" "to" *(breaking down to agonized wail)* *(sniffs)* "you."
Chester	*(Coming in slow)* Millie, what now…
Millie	I can't say it. I – I can't. Here, read it.

(Steps running away.) (Paper sounds.)

Chester	"I want to *(coughs)* VIOLATE you." Why, I never" That girl! And ME. I—had no she cared for me at…
Jo	*(Approaching)* What are you putting in your pocket?
Chester	It's personal. Just a request for me.
Jo	Let's walk along now. That Millie's crazy. They put her away and gave her head shocks. What are you doing wasting the last of the day – I'm going.
Chester	I'm sorry Jo. It's something rather sensitive that she wrote to me. I can't share it. It's something rather – special. I'm flattering in an odd way.
Jo	Hm. *(walking sound.)*
Chester	Look who's following.

(Meows)

Jo	I knew he would. 'The only animal God couldn't harness.' Humph. But if you dance 'em …
Chester	They follow.
Jo	Yes Chester.
Chester	I hope he never dies.
Jo	We all leave our bodies. Twelve years is old for a cat.
Chester	You always lecture when I say what I hope.
Jo	Where are you going?
Chester	Millie… I've GOT to answer her note.
Jo	She's off crying someplace telling her latest hysterical complaint.
Chester	*(Disappointed)* Oh.
Jo	You can find her later on the way back… oh, no.

(Sound of man's steps approaching)

Chester	Too late.
Rev	*(Unctuous)* Chester and Josephine. Out for a walk.

Jo	You don't need to be any genius, Father, to see that.
Chester	Excuse us, we…
Rev	I myself am –
Jo	If we stop now, Father, we won't get back to cut the beef liver.
Rev	*(Gently)* Stop. Stop.
Chester	No, not now Reverend. Not this late.
Rev	Do we really hear the other – what they say.
Jo	Millie's up ahead. Why not catch up with her.
Chester	She thinks I turned her down by now, I guess.
Jo	Somebody wants Millie to do something *(pause)* upsetting.
Rev	*(Rattled)* My children … being a person is upsetting, but God in his mercy … what did she tell you?
Jo	She wrote a note saying somebody said something awful.
(Overlap)	
Chester	*(Paper sound)* She has I wish. I cannot share. It's personal.

Jo   Imagine with her shape, roaming away from ANYBODY.

Chester   I thought – I thought ... I know I'm a bit short for my height, but I thought - I thought for a moment she was trying to tell me something.

Jo   She was, Chester. She was trying to tell us what happened.

(Meowing)

Chester   No, I mean... tell <u>me</u> something.

Rev   Give me the note, Chester. It'll do us no good to carry trash *(Voice rising)* she's a tart – always was and always will be - wiggling her rear when she walks, disgracing the church- it's a sin alright. Someone ought to stop her alright. *(Prayer intonation)* If God had wanted parts of our body to move he'd have put... put motors on them *(getting upset)* Her and her chicken cooking contests, getting the county all excited. Proposing such art forms. Have we ever gotten a taste of it yet? Any of us? Have we?

Jo   Caraway seeds.

Chester   Shh. Don't interrupt at a time like this, Jo.

Jo	Chicken and caraway seeds. It's been her dream. That's why she wants to promote this cooking contest of hers, to show off, I'll wager.
Rev	Don't wager, child, compounding our fallacies.
Jo	I won't, Father.
Chester	Compounding our fallacies?
Rev	Don't doubt, son.
Chester	I won't, Father.
Rev	Now *(Deep breath)* I'll be on my way ... Chester.
Chester	Yes.
Rev	Chester and Joe, let us not be too hard on Millie. Love is an important commodity. She is confused ... Don't judge her, she is not what one calls an easy lady. She takes to bed with amnesia this time every fall. We must protect her self respect. Her self respect. *(Importantly)* It's a bird that comes to call and flies on. *(Sternly)* Give me the note.

(Paper tears)

Chester	*(Coughing and gulping. Choking.)* I don't have it. There. I swallowed it. It was personal.

Jo	Are you stark raving? Swallowing paper that way! You know what ruffage does to you, tear you up. You won't even eat greens. Paper indeed. And pencil on it too. Lead poisoning is what you'll get.
Rev	Your cat. That eye blinks on and off like a diamond, hiding like that - or glass blinking on and off *(hurries away.)* Ugly animal hiding in the bush.
Jo	Humph – caraway seed in her chicken. That woman's daft. *(Pause)* Why Ches – you're crying.
Chester	It just got stuck midway down, that's all.
Jo	No Chester. You're trembling all over.
Chester	Jo, I know how you feel about body contact but would you … could you hold me in your arms for a minute?
Jo	Right here and now? Outside the way we are?
Chester	We are where we are, Jo.
Jo	That's precisely what I mean.
Chester	I think he's got a grasshopper over there, or an ant.
Jo	There are no ants out on Sunday – they're workers.

Chester	Grasshopper then.
Jo	We should be getting back now. We were to feed him the liver.
Chester	Right here and now, Jo. We could spread the blanket and lie on it. Look. I could make a bed of leaves. *(Sounds of leaves.)*
Jo	Damp leaves.
Chester	Leaves nevertheless.
Jo	I – I don't know – You're confusing me, acting like this.
Chester	What are we waiting for, Jo. Death? Is that what? Are we waiting for death to appreciate…
Jo	Well it's not that. It's – you want me to lie here? And hold you in my arms? I'm embarrassed. Someone could be coming by.
Chester	*(Groans)* Oh.
Jo	What in the world?
Chester	My stomach.
Jo	Gas.
Chester	Pain.

Jo	The note.
Chester	Phew. I'm sweating. Got stuck mid-center, it did.
Jo	No blueberries on your cheesecake tonight, none whatsoever – and don'tbeg.
Chester	I guess it was a poor idea.
Jo	Which one?
Chester	Lying down here. Chilly and all, lying down so close to the ground.

(Long meow like a howl in the distance, like a dog howling.)

	The cold could come through any blanket or tablecloth.
Jo	I never brought the cloth, Chester.
Chester	No? Nor the supper.
Jo	Never did.
Chester	Well that settles it then. Let's get the cat and go home to feed him.
Jo	*(Steps walking away) (voice from the distance)* Chester!
Chester	Coming!

Jo	Chester.
Chester	*(Distance)* God in his mercy!
Jo	Not asleep is he?
Chester	Not asleep. Not outside like this, Josephine. They don't go to sleep outside, especially when they're taking a walk.
Jo	Dead then.
Chester	Dead as his blood.
Jo	Oh. OOOOOOOh-oooooh-ooooo, Ahhhh Ahhh *(moans in agony as if rocking with the sound).*
Chester	Something he ate likely.
Jo	*(Screaming as if muted through hands.)*
Chester	Come along now, Jo. We'll get a plastic bag and come back for him.
Jo	Uh-uh-uh *(short grunts of pain.)*
Chester	We could pretend we dreamed him.
Jo	*(Sniffling)*
Chester	We could pretend he dreamed us, if it'll be a comfort to you.

Jo	*(Deep sigh)* I'm better, Chester.
Chester	Good now. Good, lady. Up-up on your feet, lady. I'll fix our dinner.
Jo	Wash your hands first, Chester.
Chester	I will, of course I will, being outside and all.
Jo	It's too much responsibility having a cat.
Chester	It's a constant worry.
Jo	He sounds like a siren, you know, that goes off.
Chester	It'll be queer in the yard.
Jo	We could call each other from across the yard and meow *(getting excited)* just for a time, not for always.
Chester	Well now, I don't know if I could.
Jo	Not loud, nothing so splendid as loud.
Chester	But even still.
Jo	Just for a time. Just until we get used to being without him.
Chester	Oh my God, here's Millie coming, and us in our grief... Down, down behind the hedge. *(Sounds of greenery.)*

(Steps approaching. Steps rushing by.)

Jo   That was close. *(Snorts)* Here and her chicken and caraway seeds.

Chester   *(Groans)*

Jo   Sorry – I forgot your tum tum. Up and off we go. He won't be in the black chair you know, ever again, or on the stair, or on the desk…

Chester   *(Meows)*

Jo   Or *(voice fades with steps as they walk away)* on the cushions. He used to sniff my breath, the cat did, especially after cinnamon toast. I think he had a secret craving *(Chester meows)* for sweets. I always thought *(Chester meows) (winding up)* it cried for me. In the garden, in the rain, it'll want to be let up but what can we do? The house will feel larger, a needless worry, cats *(meows)* We can keep each other cheerful. Living people can *(Voice and meows are heard from further away)* be an asset to one another … *(barely heard)*

(Wind, leaves sound)

THE END

Anna Nicole: Blonde Glory

Anna Nicole: Blonde Glory

by Grace Cavalieri

***

Characters:

Anna	30's	Sensual blonde wears kimono, shift Beneath for changes
Pushkin (Push)	20's-30's	Intellectual, wears sweater, collegiate, attractive
Horshel (Hors)	40's-50's	Anna's manager dressed in unkempt suit
Anima/dead twin	30's	Petite, dark hair, the opposite of Anna, wears red wings
Interviewer/Doctor	Any age	Adult male with camera Act 1, stethoscope in Act 2

ACT 1

Anna, Pushkin and Horshel. Anna gets up from chaise lounge. Toy box on floor.

Anna   Hey guys. I just had the worst dream. (*while trying to recall*) I was driving, always driving, and it was getting too dark, and I was running out of gas, and it was getting dark, and on Sunday no gas stations are open at night, and I had to go to the bathroom so I stopped to buy some candy. I saw a man dressed like Santa Claus, and he took off his boots and hat, then his belt, then all his clothes and then he said to "hug him" because he was Santa Claus. I didn't know what to do so I did.

Push   You did what?

Anna   (*Sleepily*) I hugged him! A naked Santa (*she shivers*) It was awful. (*Rummages in toy box.*) I seem to have lost something. Do you know what I lost? It was right here. And everything I almost know, I forget. It could be here (*Comes up with stuffed dog.*) OH DEAR Randy. (*Kisses dog*) (*Throws back.*)

Push   Time for your tutorial Anna.

Hors   You're becoming a problem, Pushkin. I'll give you 15 minutes, then you can shove your thesis up your…

Anna	(*Interrupting*) OH LOOK! (*Picks up tequila bottle from toy box. Holds up, looks inside, shakes upside down*) Why is Tequila always empty? (*Throws back in box.*)

Push and Hors move forward, talk to audience while Anna plays with her possessions. She picks up tiara from box. Looks in mirror, tries on froufrou throws back. Push and Horshel talk past her to audience.

Push	(*To audience*) Gentleman of the Committee: Let us say, Anna was damaged by gender. Some women are intelligent, yes. Anna… Anna is on the verge of intelligence. Thus my study.
Anna	(*To audience*) I think I know what's going on. Do you know what's going on?
Hors	(*Disgusted*) Anna is a financial liability. Like I tell her, Anna, you can't pray for people to love you. You can't bring out a statue of Madonna and her back up boys and kneel down to her and pray, and suddenly know how to dance.
Anna	Hey, guys, I'm still here.
Push	Dear Advisors … whatever moral judgments you bring here, whatever your tribunal, remember Anna's dilemma. First, she had no family or real childhood – no companionship. So what possibly could be her redemption?
Hors	I tell her, you got to make the stage your life. It's a chat room every minute. Chatter,

	chatter, chatter. Anna, please do something. An artist doesn't care what the world thinks. Pull your skirts up. The screen, the TV ... all a parade of people after people after people. Who cares? But some one person watching you on TV will stop and look and say, "Now SHE is something special!" What does it mean to have everyone in the world know you? Everything! That's what!
Anna	Can I please say something?
Push	Human behavior that begins with fright, results in splintered vision. Deprivation is on trial here, if you insist on judging Anna, at least love her. And if you ask why I cannot love her, it is because I love knowledge more: literature, philosophy, linguistics, science, and ethics, better than her – or anyone, for that matter.
Anna	(*Looks up*) And I really am afraid of death, you guys. Tell them that too while you're at it.
Push	(*To audience*) There is a black box in the lab at Princeton University made up of distorted mirrors. If you look into it, there's a photographic image. If it is someone you love, the face will not look distorted to you. Let me put it to you this way: Anna's mirror has no image whatsoever. There is a black hole always looking back at her. But, she keeps going! She is Hope itself. Bless her! Let us say, if this were the Holocaust, Anna would hang her thong on the barbed wire fence to dry.

Anna   I think I get it. I think I am beginning to.

Hors   (*To audience*) Frankly, as good as she looks – as big, as blonde – as dazzling as a drag queen at 3 A.M. – I'm told by my clients that her sex just lacks conviction. Whatever you think of her – whatever you think of me – Without me she'd be just one more ice cube in hell.

Anna   Oh I get it. An ice cube in Hell melts ... I figured that out. Right Push? You're the professor. And HORSHEL! *(coquettish)* I am not going to HELL!

Hors   You got 5 minutes with her Pushkin. Then it's show time (*exiting.*)

Push   It's always show time with you.

Anna   I'm not going to hell, but I'm afraid of heaven. I'm worried about it.

Push   Heaven? Is that what worries you? My dissertation on you is already overdue. Past due. Late. Do you hear me? Between you and your manager, I'm the one who should worry!

Anna   I am not just a bug under your microscope, Push …. Think of this. If I am here and if I get depressed, I got my pills, my vodka. But if something goes wrong in heaven ... I'm a goner.

Push   Look Anna I am praying for you, okay?

Anna   Why can't I ask my own self?

Pushkin   Oh Anna, how innocent you are. I have to be the one to interpret what God says, and I will tell you what to do. Listen to me. I have advanced degrees.

Anna   Well, what does God say?

Push   (Listens) That I, not Horshel ... I should tell you what to do. That an academic knows more than a manager (Looks at watch) OMYGOD. My Orals! (Exiting)

Anna   Yeah. Your orals. I hate to hurt your feelings but you're not very good at that. Maybe school can help.

(Horshel yells from offstage: "Anna look alive, Press is here") Interviewer rushes in with camera. Flashes of lights (With each question Anna strikes a different pose)

Interviewer   So where were you born, Anna?

Anna   In a trailer.

Interviewer   A trailer?

Anna   Double wide.

Interviewer   I mean what state.

Anna   Texas.

Interviewer	That's a big place.
Anna	Yes. There was a school with hot trees around it.
Interviewer	Where?
Anna	There was a lot of dust in the school yard. But we moved around a lot.
Interviewer	Is it true it was Beverly Hills, Texas?
Anna	I call it that, yeah.
Interviewer	Any street signs you can remember? This is for the Global Inquiry. Think, Anna. People want to picture you at home.
Anna	*(Trying)* There was... um... an old car in the yard, and... um... a refrig on the porch, and... um... OH! There was this big old colored rainbow that came out after it rained. It was so beautiful – all glowing. That's where I lived. I loved the colors in the mist so much.
Interviewer	Well thanks, that pins it down. What did you want, say, when you were 5 years old?
Anna	I think I just wanted to make it to 6. I got beaten up so much. I got on my parents' nerves.

Interviewer	There's a rumor you lost a child once. Any truth to that?
Anna	(*Flares*) That is a dirty rotten filthy lie. I got one son. A beautiful grown man-child. He's coming to visit me any day now.
Interviewer	So what do you want now Anna?
Anna	Oh I want to be happy, very, very happy, and then I'll fit my career in around that.
Interviewer	(*Exiting*) You know what? I hope you get it, Anna. You're a sweet kid. A really sweet kid.
Anna	(*Touched*) I think he liked me. (*Calling*) HORSCHEL ... He liked me. I think ….

(In jumps Anima)

Anima	I hate it when you start lying in public.
Anna	Then where should I do it? (*Confused*) Wait! I was not lying. Our parents beat the shit out of me every day and you know it.
Anima	Angels don't like dirty laundry, Anna. HOW did you get in my room again? Leave me alone, PLEASE. Hors! Pushkin! Help.
Anima	They can't see me honey, so go embarrass yourself – go ahead, make my eternity.
Anna	You seem to forget. You are dead.

Anima	Right.
Anna	You died at birth. You DIED at birth!
Anima	Yup. Our mother will never forgive you for being the one left.
Anna	My identical twin (*shudders*). I can't believe it.
Anima	(*Dryly*) As close as they could get.
Anna	Why can't you stay dead? Just this once, please. I'm on my way to something big. I want this job so much, Horshel has an audition set for me.
Anima	Now what exactly is it that you want so fucking bad?
Anna	I have a dream.
Anima	A dream? A dream!! She has a dream!
Anna	Why not? (*Flash of anger*) Even birds have dreams.
Anima	About worms. Birds dream about worms.
Anna	Maybe that's true, but it's their dreams and they have a right. Listen, I'm going to audition for the Hippodrome, and if you could just this once not get in my way, nothing personal against you – but I need this chance to show

	my stuff, to show that I can sing and dance. That I'm more than a PETA spokesperson.
Anima	Sure. I think I can help.
Anna	NO. No thanks! No help. Just like, go someplace. A vacation for a while ….
Anima	No can do. But I can stay and help.
Anna	Anima I'm begging you this time. I am scared. I am really, really scared.
Anima	OK. First, here's a little pill (*hands pill bottle*). Take it.
Anna	Another little pill? That's what you've been giving me, and after a while I always wind up in a room as big as a cell.
Anima	Oh, before, that was just so you'd have fun, for recreation. This is to give you confidence.
Anna	Confidence.
Anima	You know the stuff other people have, mostly important men. Where they can say and do anything and not feel ashamed, even after they're exposed on TV for whatever they did wrong.
Anna	(*Thoughtful*) Not feel ashamed?

Anima	Would be great, yes? (*Pours pills into Anna's hand*)
Anna	But Anima, I don't get it … (*Looks at hand*) If I'm scared before I take the pills, and then after I take the pills, I'm not scared … then who am I? Which person?
Anima	(*Sweetly*) The one who doesn't feel shame after.
Anna	Ok I'll try … (*swallows handful – flops down*)
Anima	And for the sake of decency, when you sit down keep your skirt between your legs. Angels don't like crotches.
Anna	You know that interviewer liked me. I know he did. And I was so happy and just when everything goes so good … then you (*Looks at pills*) … and so what do you want from me? For these? People keep giving me stuff I don't want to get something from me I don't want to give. This keeps happening to me.
Anima	(*Anima exits*) Angels don't like complaints.
Anna	(*Jumps up runs after*) Wait, wait ANIMA! COME BACK. How many pills do I take to not feel shame? HELP. What do I do with these? WHEN? COME BACK. HELP. (*She goes to each corner calling her back.*) COME HERE THIS MINUTE. You can't leave me like this.

Enter Horshel

Hors What the hell is all this screaming about? *(Accusingly)* Drugs?!

Anna No thanks Horshel. I have some.

Hors Get up and look alive. I have it!

Anna You have what?

Hors Pop Porn! I may have a backer. The product. For YOU. To put your name in every TV room. Something people can eat while they watch you on TV. POP PORN! They put it in the microwave while they watch you having sex on video.

Anna Buttered? That is fattening. You wanted me to lose weight. It's not even real butter and the salt isn't even …

Hors Anna, this is what we need. A product we can sell besides your body. Something people can chew on besides your body. Something with a fragrance.

Anna Besides my body. I don't know ….

Hors Imagine it on every shelf in the video store.

Anna *(Excitedly)* Blockbusters?

Hors	Um ... No not that one. Some other ones. I am wild with the idea. I have to call the graphics people.
Anna	Do we kitchen test it? And I talk about it then? On TV? In an apron?
Hors	Not your worry, my little flower. We just need your photo on the bag.
Anna	I have a beautiful idea for a picture.
Horshel	Breasts. A picture of your breasts.
Anna	I was thinking of boats. I like happy boats.
Hors	No Anna.
Anna	Sailors would like it.
Hors	Breasts.
Anna	With happy boats in the background and maybe a sun?
Hors	Just the breasts Anna, POP PORN. You will be famous yet!
Anna	I'm not too sure about the picture on the bag.
Hors	Breasts Anna, which one of us lived near a college, me or you?
Anna	I'm not sure about this, Hors.

Hors	*(Whips out a box from his jacket)* A present. Let us say a little persuasion packet.
Anna	For me?
Horshel	There's no one else here stupid, of course for you. *(Anna pulls out a huge ugly seashell on a chain).*
Anna	Oh (He puts it around her neck) (weight slumps her)
Hors	What do you have to say about it?
Anna	Oh I like it.
Hors	Is that all you have to say? Use your words, Anna.
Anna	Oh I really like it.
Hors	And that chain? That connects ME to YOU, forever.
Anna	Hors? Hors ...
Hors	What now? You've been fighting me all day.
Anna	I can tell you're mad at me, Horshel. Did I do something wrong last night after meeting those rich producers?

Hors	Anna, next time, please do not say ANYHOO when asked about world affairs.
Anna	Did I eat ok at the restaurant? I loved that white satin table cloth.
Hors	And no ketchup on the Kobe beef next time. Please Anna? for God's Sake! (*He leans over and shouts in her ear*) That meal cost those suits a fortune!
Anna	Your breath is on my shoulder (*She wipes it away*)
Hors	You are on your way to nowhere fast Anna. (*Pause*) You slept with that security guard from the restaurant, didn't you?
Anna	He said he needed a place to practice. He was from a foreign country and didn't know the language and ...
Hors	Anna, you know you came from nothing and I can send you back. Can you sing? No. Can you dance? No. Can you act? No. You are not thin and you are not even nice. You can't do anything. That's why you need an agent.
Anna	Why do you always describe me by what I CANNOT do? (*Strongly*) Okay I can't sing but I can hum.
Hors	Well I have a job for you. (*Freeze Hors*) (*Enter interviewer*)

(Anna drops her robe, a pose, lights go off. Mic in her face)

Interviewer   What do you think when you're naked, Anna?

Anna   I don't think. *(Profoundly)* You are what you think. Professor Pushkin told me that.

Hors   *(Hisses) (Indicates interviewer)* Edit yourself Anna!

Interviewer   How do you think you look nude, Anna?

Anna   Happy? Is that the answer? Very happy.

Interviewer   If you don't mind.

Anna   I don't mind.

Interviewer   I'd like to ask something personal. Why do you wear so much makeup?

Anna   Well, Horshel says I'm better off if my makeup does the acting for me.

Hors   *(Hors pulls her away roughly)* That's enough boys. Later. 3pm. Later.

Interviewer   *(Protesting)* Goddam. We were just getting started. Goddam these handlers *(Exit)*

Hors   *(To Anna)* Until we get your food product started, I got another job for you *(Shakes paper in her face)*. Something just came

	through. If you are nice, this guy can fund your name brand.
Anna	Wonderful. See Hors, I told you if you had faith I me …

(Hors shows her a cheerleader outfit. Hands her pom poms.)

Anna	*(Anna holds up skirt to herself)* There are no pants.
Hors	It's not what you think.
Anna	It's probably worse.
Hors	There is this old guy who likes football but he likes live cheerleaders when he watches TV. You just have to jump up and down when a team scores. Any team.
Anna	Jump Up?
Hors	AND down.
Anna	I need to get in shape.
Hors	Yes Anna. We'll give you this gig, but if you can't lose weight I'm hanging my car over the top of the Empire State Building with you on the passenger side. With the door open.
Anna	*(Whimpering)* Which side is the Empire State Building? *(Starts sniffling)*

Hors	You do this one thing and you'll have so many jobs you'll have to sleep with your shoes on. (*Exit Hors*) Now get dressed, I'll leave you to yourself.
Anna	Oh no, not to myself.

(Enter Anima)

Anima	Don't worry sweetheart, you'll never be alone.

(Anna picks toy dog Randy up from doll bed)

Anna	Once I had this little doggie, Anima. I rescued him from the house that burned down. I saw something move. It was so dirty, and I picked it up and held it.

(Hors calls offstage: TIME TO GO ANNA)

Anna	And I fed the little mutt and kept it on a leash in the yard. This puppy loved me.
Anima	*(To audience)* If she says her father shot him don't believe her. He ran away. She almost kissed him to death that's why.
Anna	Well he did shoot him. Right in front of me, and if I die Randy is waiting for me. In Heaven. That's the only reason I want to go there. I want to so bad.
Hors	*(Peeks in)* I'm waiting for you in the green room and you're spinning a tale?! The

	producer's waiting. You think we're paying you by the pound?
Anima	You have an interview at 3pm, and no family secrets or you'll be sorry.
Anna	I don't tell secrets. And I just think I would like to commit suicide today, if you will please excuse me. I cannot do pop porn and cheerleading and my audition and a photo shoot and dance practice and all these things at once.
Anima	I will take your dolls away if I hear one more word of suicide. How would that look to the world? I'd like to remind you what you've done to your family. The time you tried to drink Clorox and we had to pay good money to have your stomach pumped. The time you tried suicide and jammed your new Ford Pinto into a tree and the poor medics had to work an hour drilling the doors open.
Anna	I made it up to them. Both of them. Twice.
Anima	Naturally our father broke your arm and you ruined our whole Christmas day. When our brother's friend (*makes quote marks with hands*) "Raped" you, you had to shoot your big mouth all over the town. We could not show our faces after that. Well, that will never happen again. You have caused nothing but trouble.

Anna	Actually, I AM going to kill myself. I just don't know when.
Anima	That does it! If you do that, then how could I possibly reach you when I need your help? No one had a more ungrateful sister. (*Exiting*) I'm leaving you alone.
Anna	(*Frightened*) I'll be good. Don't go.
Anima	(*Exiting*) Remember this Anna, we loved you. Your family loved you. Do you want to be left all alone? Do you?
Anna	I'll be good (*Anna cuddles her toy dog. Interviewer rushes in). Runs across stage. Camera flashes off. Anna strikes a pose holding her breasts up then flops back dejected*)
Interviewer	(*Exiting*) SHE IS GOOD man, she is Very Very Good! (*Crosses stage)(Out*)

(*Anna gets stuffed dog and holds it to her. She cuddles up and puts her face in its fur, rocking gently*)

Anna	(*There is a hypo needle behind Randy's collar, Anna pulls out*) Want a kiss Randy? Randy, do you want some heroin? Randy. Did you know they call heroin HORSE, Randy? You want to ride a horse, Randy? (*Kissing the stuffed toy*) You'll like it. Blanked out. That's how it feels. Like that chair. You feel like that chair over there. Nothing. That's what we want Randy. If you're a man you can be a smart person, but a

	girl has to get a job to go anywhere. I always thought I'd find a man to love, and have a new baby, but the baby could die someday. That's why I love you Randy. You don't die. Help me, Randy *(howls) (Looks to inject in her arm, then plunges it into Randy)* I NEED HELP, HEEELLLLPP.
Push	*(Rushes in)* Anna I'm back. What's the matter? Who are you talking to?
Anna	*(Throws Randy aside) (Covering up)* Help. I need help Pushkin, I need YOUR help ah … ah … I want to learn *(thinking)* big words. You said you'd help me.
Push	This is admirable Anna. I'm happy to hear the outrage of your past is overcoming the present. Of course you do, and you deserve to. I'll teach you one thing a day. This is splendid *(Notes it in his book)* Okay, you start. Ask ME a question. Anything.
Anna	Where am I? *(Wiping her tears away)* Oh Pushkin, where in the hell am I?
Push	Why does that matter? You're home. Try to get a sense of yourself in a sense of place.
Anna	Well I get a better sense of myself when I'm AWAY from home, because when I'm home I think I AM home, but since I don't really have a sense of it, it's better to be away from it.

Push	Let's get back to work Anna. I want to help you.
Anna	You could really help me if you wanted, Pushkin. I want that audition Pushkin, I want to be somebody.
Push	Oh good, good. Do you know who?
Anna	Anybody. Just somebody not like I am.
Push	Well, first an artist must be courageous and not care what anyone else thinks.
Anna	Oh that's me alright. I went out shopping without underwear, and when I got out of the limo I didn't care how they shot the picture.
Push	There's more than that.
Anna	(*Disappointed*) I showed as much as I could.
Push	We are still in phase one of your learning capacity. (*Leafs through folder*) Now, I asked you about World World War II yesterday. Our lesson for the day: Hitler. And you were to come up with a reaction. "It's terrific" does not cut it! When are you going to think Anna? Think.
Anna	Well whose side were we on in World War II?
Push	We won Anna, that is all that counts.

Anna	We won? Well our dead aren't more alive than their dead, so I don't get it.
Push	I'm going to take away the funnies and give you some good things to read, Anna. I think you have great potential, Anna, and I want to prove that.
Anna	I do not want to be a teacher, Push, I want to be a star. (*Turns away*)
Push	Talk to me Anna, don't walk away. Remember the story of Mary and Martha. Martha did all the work but Jesus says Mary sits and talks with him and she is the one to emulate. Luke: chapter 10, verse 39.
Anna	Shit, Pushkin, Martha doesn't get enough credit. She was doing all the hard work around the house. And your stories always do that. They say wrong things about wrong people.
Push	In the fullness of time you will see me as a helpmate.
Anna	Horshel says I'm a shooting star.
Push	Ah, but a shooting star is a falling star Anna.
Anna	I cannot ever do anything right! Okay? Comfuckingprendez vous?
Push	Good. You're expanding your use of language. Knowledge is about finding yourself.

Anna	*(Puzzled)* Who?
Push	There's one more thing.
Anna	Not one more thing.
Push	A gift for you and your progress. *(Gives her a necklace. Huge silver chain with a globe of the world on it. Hangs around her neck on top of Horshel's necklace.)* Do you like it?
Anna	*(Staggers)* It's really big.
Push	Is that all you have to say?
Anna	It's nice and heavy too.
Push	Now that you have a token of my affection, maybe you'll concentrate. My dissertation depends on it. Tell me, don't you ever wonder about anything? *(Taking notes)*
Anna	*(Anna stops.) (She goes to the window.)* I do. I do wonder something, Pushkin. I do. It's about birds I see. They are my only friends.
Push	Dear Anna, are you making fun of me?
Anna	No, no truly. I have always wondered, you know ... for instance ... those pretty birds that are so red? How do they get that way? Did you ever wonder about that?

Push	That's all you wonder about? Cardinals? And red feathers?
Anna	Yeah and about their dreams. What they dream of ... you know? They can't sing or dance either, so what do they dream of becoming?
Push	They dream of worms, Anna. Worms. (*Patiently*) Worms. Birds dream of worms.
Anna	Oh I was afraid you'd say that. (*Pops pill in mouth*) (*Pushkin sits her down*)
Push	This is not helpful to our endeavor. To be more complete you must memorize things. The names of Presidents for example and, Anna, please listen. Help me to help you. You have to read just one page of a book a day.
Anna	I have people that do that for me.
Push	I gave you some words yesterday do you remember?
Anna	Yes. I have them right here.
Push	Do you remember the assignment?
Anna	Of course I do. I was to think of a feeling.
Push	Yes, feeling, action, put together some creative thing from you I can live with Anna.

Anna	I love you Push. And so I was supposed to use the word "heart" and make it rhyme.
Push	A simple task.
Anna	(*Pulls paper out of her back pocket*) When I look at you (*playfully shouts*) 'my heart farts.'
Push	(*Weakly*) Mine does too, Anna. Mine does too. (*Puts his head in his arms in defeat*)
Anna	(*Squirms, puts her breast against his ear.*) (*Playfully*) Hello Push? Hello. Can you hear me? Hello, Anna calling Pushkin.
Push	(*Stiffening*) Anna I am not playing telephone today. I am trying to get you ready for something.
Anna	Me too Pushkin. Me too.
Push	(*Pushkin takes a deep breath, closes his eyes*) Anna, people see you as a bimbo. When death comes to call, what do you want to do – order a pizza? Show your rap sheet? Have you no wish for the strange and beautiful? Take your breast out of my ear this instant Anna! (*He stands. She drops back*)

(*Enter Horshel*)

Hors	I just got a call from the mansion. Why didn't you do what I said? The old guy had bucks to burn.

Anna	I couldn't Hors. I felt sick.
Hors	No excuse. When your back is to the wall is when you show your stuff.
Anna	My back is to the wall, but the wall is always on the floor with your guys.
Push	Identify from inside yourself and not outside the world, Anna. Don't listen.
Hors	This is why we don't have a relationship Anna.
Push	Obedience is not a relationship, Horshel.
Hors	You couldn't find the old guy's bedroom? It's the one with a bed.
Anna	I'm through with your goddamn clients. Pushkin says your men treat me without any trace of affection. And that I have stored up memories I have to deal with.
Hors	What are they?
Anna	Um…I forget.
Hors	Ha! You forget memories? Memories are something you remember.
Push	Find something you love Anna, so you do not cave into him. Think of something you love.

Anna	Pushkin calls my life a cockfight. Is that a nice thing to say about a girl?
Push	What do you love Anna?
Anna	Um (*thinks*) I love when they clap. *(Pause)* But clapping is supposed to make me happy, but then it makes me depressed.
Push	Remember the sad legend of Sir Gawain? He needed more and more kisses to be happy.
Hors	Life kills you - that's all you need to know Anna. I am in charge of you in the meantime. Anna, it's always the same. You say I LOVE YOU too much and guys get sick of you and leave. You always do that. You overcome men. But when you're on a PAYING job you ignore them, I can't figure you.
Anna	Pushkin says my body has had no special moments.
Hors	The more I talk to you the more I side with your family. You are ungrateful and untrustworthy. And I give you pretty things. *(Lifts her seashell lets it drop hard on her chest)* *(She winces)*
Anna	Maybe there's something pretty when you die but I want to see it first. I don't see anything pretty here in life.

Hors   Anna, take some advice, only talk when no one is listening. You'll do better.

Push   We belong to the dark, to the unknown. Believe in your own moral authority, Anna.

Hors   Sorry to interrupt Professor, you've taken up about enough of our time. *(To Anna)*. All you have to do is look at the dailies, Anna, they show us the audience response is down. Something is off with you. You have to give them what they want, Anna. The audience is like a woman, it's all in the playbook. You must manipulate it, seduce it, the audience is a girl, nothing but a girl. You have to OWN it, the audience.

(Push takes out his notebook and starts scribbling what he observes)

Anna   I just do what you say. I cannot force them to like me.

Hors   You can force your way in anyplace ... You have to knock down their doors. Demand your place. Life is a game, you gotta WIN IT. It's like playing tennis (*Push walks away in disgust*)

Anna   (*Admiringly*) I didn't know you played, Horshel.

Hors   Oh tennis is quite a game. Skill. Speed. Movement, accuracy, placing the ball just right. There was this tennis club down on 12th and Front St. A private place. They didn't let

	Jews in … So me and my friends Callahan and Bernadetti …
Anna	They got you in, Hors?
Hors	No, they couldn't get in either, so we'd wait and walk in the back of some tall guys behind them, guys who belonged, holding conversations with them, and we'd slink in behind them through the doors.
Anna	So that's how you learned to play tennis Hors?
Hors	No Dolly, we never did play tennis. Don't you get it? But we got in. That's the whole point in life. You got to get past the gate. Then we clapped for them. The tall guys who played.
Anna	But you didn't actually do it yourself?
Hors	No we couldn't, I just told you.
Anna	So I am on stage for other people so they can clap for things they cannot do themselves?
Hors	Honey you're not even past the gate yet. But in a way yes, you are living for other people. You gotta manipulate them.
Push	*(Rushes between them)* Manipulation is a position of weakness Hors, and you know it. A flight of fancy, Horshel.

Hors	I have had enough of you. This is where Push comes to shove, Pushkin. *(Shoves him hard - Push falls backward)* That's where flights of fancy land, as we say here on earth.

(Anna rushes to help Push up)

Anna	Oh Pushkin I'm so sorry. Are you hurt? Speak to me. Can you talk?
Push	*(Glasses awry, breath knocked out of him) (Long pause)* I am. Let us say I am muted by irony. My fault! Entirely my fault. I trusted evolution of the species.
Anna	What IS a flight of fancy, Push?

(Hors tries to drag her off.) (Push grabs her other arm)

Push	Anna!!! Stay here.
Hors	*(Yanks her other arm) (They are pulling her opposite directions)* ANNA!!! Come here.
Anna	I have to go with Horshel, Pushkin. He's my manager. I really really really have to.
Push	You use too many adverbs, Anna. I am trying…
Anna	What Pushkin?
Push	I am trying to protect you from growing old and becoming what you used to be.

Anna   (*Rushing to follow Horshel*) Never mind. I used to be nothing. Don't worry, Pushkin.

SCENE

Anna and Horshel (Horshel is walking around her, pacing)

Anna   I think I'm making progress in school, Horshel. And Pushkin seems to like me.

Hors   You have 3 days before the screen-test and what are you doing with that guy, studying Greek?

Anna   Hors, I've been practicing. Look at the blisters on my heels. (*Shows*) I keep trying and …

Hors   You have to dance faster Anna, You have to keep them interested, shake that fanny Anna, give them breast!

Anna   I swear there's no pay off. I get up early to practice and at night I'm no faster.

Hors   (*Waxing eloquently*) You're looking for a payoff Anna? A PAYOFF? There is no payoff in life … it's just keeping on keeping on. I found out early. When I was a boy my mother made me drink a glass of milk before every meal before I could eat and I swore when I grew up I'd be free – but you know what? I can't sit down and eat without a glass of fucking milk first and I hate it. I hate it. I'm just used to it. I have to do it. There's no escape. There's no

	end to it Anna. Look at it this way. You swim in the mud your whole life and then you die and you're under it. No payoffs.
Anna	I think I understand Horshel. I want to do good. I do. I want people to see me as something other than myself – I'm really really just a nice person, who likes animals and small children, that's a terrible image for a star.
Hors	Right! Get busy, and keep it FAST, your dance. We don't want people going to the bar while you're doing your act. KEEP IT FAST.
Anna	(*Sings lyrics*) What good are my furbelows /and my little tippy toes/ if I'm not with my baaaby/
Hors	Good. This time with music.

(*Music starts*)

ANNA	(B*ellows like blues singer. Charleston dance steps*) WHAT GOOD ARE MY FURBELOWS OR MY LITTLE TIPPPIE TOES IF I'M NOT WITH MY BABY …. (*She tries again faster. Turns her back toward audience and shakes it. Shakes her breasts. Winks over shoulders*) (*opens robe*) (*Hors gives her thumbs up and exits*) (*Anna does it one more time. Trying to move feet daintily*) (*Anna does number again*) (*sings line 2*) What good is a tiny nose, lips just like the reddest rose, if I'm not with my baaaaby …

(Music winds down. Halts abruptly.)

Anna	*(stops)* What happened?
Anima	(*Enters*) Oh Anna, Anna ... I just saw Horshel.
Anna	Yeah, I did too. He just left.
Anima	He was watching just now. Through the studio window. Your second try.
Anna	Oh yeah? How'd I do (*she starts shaking again*) He likes? *(Anima shakes her head slowly)*
Anna	*(Shakes her head slowly in imitation)* No?
Anima	No.
Anna	NO? He didn't like it?
Anima	Oh it's not that he didn't like it, he LOVED it.
Anna	He did?
Anima	But I heard him mutter. Just too fast. Too damn fast.
Anna	He told me to go faster ... I almost skinned my damn heels.
Anima	Well ... you know how proud men are.
Anna	How proud?

Anima	He admitted just now that it looked silly fast. He was wrong about the tempo. It's not in keeping with your dignity.
Anna	He said that? *(Pleased)* My dignity? Oh that means a lot to me, coming from him.
Anima	Yup, too proud to talk to you himself, I thought I'd do it for him. Then we can surprise him when you get it right.
Anna	I don't believe you.
Anima	Ok I'll get it in writing. (*Anna keeps steps, clumsily practicing dancing*)

(Anima rushes out and writes on big poster board TOO DAMN FAST.)

Anima	(*Returns to Anna*) Here it is in writing.
Anna	*(Reads)* Too damn fast. That's what he says, all right! Too Fast. Well, maybe he can't admit he was wrong. Knowing I worked so hard, all these days.
Anima	Let's try it halftime, baby. I'm your sister. I am the other half of you. Sisters know best.

(Anna shudders at the thought. Music is reduced to a drone)

Anna	What good are my tippy toes and my little furbelows if I'm not with my baby. (*Singing it off tune like a lounge song*)

Anima   Slower honey, let them savor you. Milk the notes. Ride the vowels. Drape yourself.

(Anna enunciates each vowel, painfully slow) (Drapes herself across chair)

Anima   Better. Better.

Anna   Are you sure? I'm scared.

Anima   Of course honey. Here. Take a pill. *(Hands her pill bottle.)* We want that sleepy look in a songster's eyes, that velvety tone, that come hither purr.

(Anna, slurring, sings again. Anna takes more pills. Overdoing, leaning forward, each note hands on knees).

Anima   *(Talking in her ear)* I think you're getting it ... Do it just like that. You'll get a big big reaction from Horshel! See Anna. You are a product and we are your advertisers. We advertise you the right way and people are made agitated by the advertising and feel if they satisfy their appetites with you the anxiety will go away, but first you must show them a need to feel anxious so they will feel better by coming to see you perform.

Anna   *(Dreamlike)* Well why do we want to cause all that trouble? Why can't we just let people alone to choose for themselves? *(Anna curls up on chaise lounge.)*

(Exit Anima)

SCENE

*(Push and Max **both** enter)*

Push   I had to call you in Horshel. I know I'm not supposed to interfere, but look. Pretty pathetic. Look at what you've done, Horshel. The poor kid is passed out. You're messing her up Horshel, with all your pressure. Shouting orders. Insulting her. Every time you put someone down you stunt their growth.

Hors   She's taller than I am by two inches.

Pushkin   I mean her emotional growth.

Hors   She has a life.

Push   Not an emotional life. You control that. She is like a child.

Hors   She came to me and said she wanted to be changed. I'm changing her.

Push   Conformed is not transformed.

Hors   Whatever that is.

Push   And don't end a sentence with IS.

Hors	(*Points finger in Push's face*) And don't start a sentence with DON'T.
Push	When you control a person's actions and feelings, that is DEATH. It is taking the horn off the unicorn. It's turning a shooting star into rock.
Hors	She gets love 24/7. How many women can say that? Other men's dreams and desires – all hers.
Push	Love turns to hate, you'll see Horshel, and you can't hold her.
Hors	It turns right back to love when we turn off her giant screen TV's. Money is the bible we use, Professor Pushkin. (*Anna awakes*)
Anna	I heard a dream of the highest star. Pushkin come listen. Here. Listen. (*Listens to seashell at her ear.*)
Pushkin	Come on Anna. You're on commercial break. Let's get out of here and get some dinner.
Hors	Be back in an hour, Anna, and if you don't get your part down by tonight we're going to save a bundle of money on your wardrobe because no one is going to come see you. I'll be back. (*Exits*)

SCENE

(Anna and Pushkin back from restaurant)

Pushkin	Now's your chance Anna. He's not back yet. You can go. Run, Anna. You can leave and never come back.
Anna	I cannot leave him … (*Push removes seashell from her neck. Hands it to her*)
Push	His chain is off.
Anna	(*Sigh*) But he needs me.
Push	He'll survive without you. Like any reptile in the desert.
Anna	He depends on me. I'm his bread and butter. He told me so. But Pushkin, it's you I love Push. You must know that's why I agreed to study with you. I've already learned everything I need to know.
Anna	(*Removes coat. Puts on kimono*) I love you so much.
Push	(*Removes cravat, collar open*) You've said that before.
Anna	Pushkin! Why is it you don't want sex with me?
Push	It's pretty animalistic.

Anna	I thought you liked animals.
Push	I like to study them Anna, and count them. I am an anthropologist.
Anna	Oh but remember how you told me about animals and mating seasons.
Push	Sex has its place as instructive and emblematic of humankind, yes. You see Anna, because I am an intellectual I only get an erection once a year.
Anna	Well I love you Pushkin, and I understand that is the way intellectuals are then.
Push	I confess today I received an erected condition.
Anna	(*Anna starts to drop her robe*)
Push	But I used it already.
Anna	(*Retrieves robe*) Oh Push. Why?
Push	Please don't be sad, but I'm not sexually attracted to you Anna.
Anna	Not to put you on the spot but I was just wondering why?
Push	Well you're very lovely but, I don't know, you are unfinished somehow.

Anna	You could have saved some of yourself for me anyway Pushkin. Just to be friendly.
Push	Anna, I gotta run.
Anna	Do you think you'll get another erection some time soon?
Push	I do not know Anna. It depends on exams and stress and research. *(He tries to exit)*
Anna	One more thing. About tonight? At the restaurant. It was lovely but …
Push	How was it lovely, Anna? The food? Ambiance? Expand your locution.
Anna	Pushkin why did you have to touch her hair?
Push	Who?
Anna	The waitress. Why did you have to touch the waitress's hair?
Push	I love women. I love their clothes, everything about them. I love the very IDEA of women.
Anna	So you have to stop and talk to everyone that passes?
Pushkin	*(Laughingly)* I like it that they'll go away.
Anna	So you like to talk to them so they'll go away?

Push	No I like that I don't have to do anything after talking to them. Don't you see?
Anna	But the waitress. You touched her hair.
Push	I like blond hair.
Anna	I have blonde hair.
Push	I like blonde hair that I don't have to take home.
Anna	Every night I dream I'm with a man I WANT to be with, not HAVE to be with, and in my dream, right before he comes to me, he disappears.
Push	You can control your dreams. It is a known fact. Science proved that.
Anna	But before we left the restaurant, you followed her into the kitchen ...
Pushkin	I needed mustard.
Anna	And you show more LOVE to perfect strangers than to me and you don't even eat mustard.
Pushkin	Gotta go. I got an exam tomorrow.
Anna	Oh yes. About that erection ... If ever ... Text me? *(Push walks away in huff.)(Enter Anima.)*
Anima	I got candy!

Anna	You know I'm supposed to be losing weight. Okay, give me some.
Anima	Want to play dolls?... snort some coke?... jump on the bed?
Anna	Pushkin rejected me for good this time. No Anima, go away I need to be alone.
Anima	Since WHEN? What do you do when you're alone anyway?
Anna	I look for people to party with.
Anima	Yeah. I can see you do need some solitude then. There's hardly a soul here to party with, but me of course.
Anna	Please Anima, why torture me? I have nothing to give you.
Anima	You got life and I got death at birth so I would say you had quite a debt going on.
Anna	I couldn't help it.
Anima	Oh NO you couldn't help it. Look at you. Big and fat and empty. I am scrawny and skinny. You got all the stuff in the belly of the whale because you were on top and wouldn't let me …

Anna	I had nothing to do with that Anima. GO or I'll call the security.
Anima	(*Roars with laughter*) Oh please do. Like last time, when they put you back in rehab. They can't see me. No one can but you because you killed me. So call away, Sis.
Anna	Okay so I killed you ... hand me the eyeliner (*Anima does it*). No, the green.
Anima	However, if you were famous and happy and RESPECTED, you could change all this.
Anna	For real?
Anima	As true as I am standing before you.
Anna	You're in back of me.
Anima	Ghosts don't give a shit – forward, backward. That's human stuff.
Anna	I am respected already.
Anima	No I mean when your clothes are ON.
Anna	What in the hell do you want from me, what do you want me to do?
Anima	I was thinking ...
Anna	Spirits don't think.

Anima   Ok I was passing through thoughts and …

Anna   Hurry up, I have to find my eyelashes.

Anima   If you played on stage, a noble figure, someone the world respected, a winner who inspired everyone, then the audience would think it was you, because audiences are that way. They think the house is really a house on stage and that the actors really feel the way they say, so, well, the audience would think YOU are the wonderful celebrity with all the integrity. And Horshel would be rich and Pushkin would fall in love with you.

Anna   I like the part already. I'll do it. Who?

Anima   I was passing through thoughts and I think the best person would be …

Anna   I'd need all new clothes.

Anima   Muhammad Ali.

Anna   Who was he?

Anima   You'll find out when you play him.

Anna   He's a man.

Anima   Theater is all deception, lies, manipulation. You'll be great.

Anna   So, I don't have to dance? My feet are raw.

Anima	Hmmm, I'll have to research that upstairs. I don't think that was his fine point.
Anna	Well what if Hors won't let me?
Anima	Oh you have to insist on it. This is your only chance for respectability and to get rid of me at the same time ... in fact it's the same thing ... you are admired, and I check out. We'll press Horshel. Say you'll marry Pushkin if he doesn't let you.
Anna	Pushkin doesn't want me.
Anima	No matter, marry him anyway. Most women just find that out later. You'll be ahead of the game.
Anna	This is all too much for my head.
Anima	*(Sing song)* You'll get rid of me.
Anna	Muhammad WHO?
Anima	Muhammad Ali, "the KING," King. Like on a throne.
Anna	Throne. I like that. I could have a tiara.
Anima	Do it tonight.
Anna	Is it night now or is it day.

Anima	If it's light, it's day.
Anna	But (*looks at watch*) 3 o'clock. How do you know if that's in the morning or at night?
Anima	3 o'clock is in the middle don't worry about it. You got me, Sis, to do the worrying and I got YOU.

(Anna takes a handful of pills then sprays perfume on her neck)

Anna	Now the pills, what time did you say I take all these?
Anima	Since you don't know what time it is, I think you can take them any time you want. The more the better.
Anna	And if I take more, maybe I'll REALLY be good enough to play Muhammad Ali. But what about fashion? I will not go on stage with no makeup.
Anima	Oh he was a black guy, very good looking with a lot of bling.
Anna	He was black?
Anima	Yup.
Anna	Is he still black?
Anima	(*Raises eyes to heaven*) I'll ask upstairs.

Anna   And also ask that part about being dead.

Anima   Yes? I know a lot about that.

Anna   I've always wondered why God went through all the trouble getting rid of live people. When he could just keep the people he already had.

Anima   I'll ask.

Anna   Also, how will everyone believe I am Muhammad Ali?

Anima   Oh easy. That's a PR trick. It's called Trumor. You just start these rumors and people start to think they're true and then you show up on stage and they're delighted that they already knew it.

Anna   (*Pensive*) Trumors.

Anima   I'm sure your handlers will love it.

Anna   I'll ask.

(*Exit Anima*) (*Knock on door*)

Anna   Whoever you are just go away please.

Interviewer (*Hesitantly moves in*) Miss Smith?

Anna   I'm not scheduled for anybody now and just get out.

Interviewer	Global Inquiry here. I don't want anything, Anna. I have something to give you.
Anna	That'll be the day.
Interviewer	My boss. (*Hands her paper*) A contract. (*Anna reads*)
Interviewer	The shots I took are beautiful, the editor says your face is radiant and he wants you on the cover. And for the centerfold.
Anna	I'm not taking my clothes off one more time. Get lost.
Interviewer	Oh no. Clothes on. We think you are an undiscovered beauty. Your face. The bones. There is innocence there Anna. We want to show it. A childlike unruined beauty. A sweet face. The world is ready for this. How you are studying with the professor to better yourself. A success story.
Anna	(*To audience*) I look better than my photos. I know I look better. They never get the light right. They make my mouth look big, my chin too fat. They swallow up cheekbones. I never saw a photo that looked like me yet. That's why I want to meet a painter. A real painter who will paint me with paints and colors the way I really look. That's why I am sad, because no one knows what I really look like. Real life is so fake. I want a painter to paint it real.

Interviewer	It will be a series of expressions. Just your wonderment. I know we can capture that. Like when you were talking about the rainbow. That look. We think we can catch the Anna not yet seen ... one the world will see for what she is. And her beauty. Her internal beauty. Her struggle to be whole. We can show that. Honey, you will finally see who you really are.
Anna	You're not making fun of me? You think I have beauty inside? And that will be in the pictures? And I keep my clothes on? And everyone will like me? And then maybe my true love will read about me? And then we would get married and I would have a baby to love?
Hors	*(Enters)* And just who let you in here?
Interviewer	I knocked.
Anna	Horshel. It finally happened. You don't have to do pop porn and we don't have to go to all that trouble finding funders. The Global wants my face and I can keep my clothes on because it gets so cold, usually and ...
Hors	*(Grabs paper)* And what the hell is this?
Anna	My contract.
Hors	You don't have the authority. You don't have a contract. *(Reads)* And you sure as hell don't have this one *(rips up)*.

Interviewer	You'll hear from me. (*Exiting*)
Hors	The old guy is getting out of the limo. Get ready Anna. We made a date with a billionaire and your time is spoken for and paid for.
Anna	He's probably just another creep that smells.
Hors	Not all men are bad, Anna.
Anna	That's true. Some are dead.
Hors	And we need one quick shoot before you go.
Anna	They were going to take a good picture of me, Horshel, for the news. With clothes on, and I would see what I really look like.

(*Enter Pushkin.*) (*Anima hands him box.*)

Push	This came at the door Anna. It's for you.
Anna	(*Still stunned by defeat*) From the nice news guy?
Anima	For you. To celebrate what you really look like.
Anna	(*Weakly*) I like presents. (*Opens*)(*There is toy dog Randy hung from a rope, Decapitated, a hypodermic stuck into him.*)
Anima	He died for your sins, Anna. (*Exits*)

(Anna drops box and sits frozen)

Hors	Now is not the time to play with your toys, Anna. Get rid of that damn dog. Anna, listen up. And listen now. Get ready. The photographer's here. Get naked.
Anna	Where? (*She starts to disrobe*)
Hors	Just where it counts.
Push	(*Pulls clothes up*) NO, you cover up, Anna.
Anna	Where?
Push	Just where it counts.
Hors	Hurry up.
Pushkin	Hurry up. Our tutorial.
Anna	Never mind, Pushkin. I'm just a ... a trumor.
Hors	(*Horshel exiting*) Make it fast. (Shouts offstage) Put the old guy in the green room. (To Anna) And fix your damn face Anna.

FADE TO BLACK

ACT 2

SCENE

Anna in court room sitting on chair on dais (Hors and Push on either side of her)(Anima on stool looking down)

Anna (*Sniffling in hankie*) I loved him, he was the kindest man I ever knew, the only father I ever knew, and he chose me! Him, with all his money and cars, chose me, calling me "Anna his little angel of itching," meaning I made him itch where he couldn't scratch. Isn't that sweet? My lawyer says this should not have to go to trial. He was my husband and he loved me and left me his money. That's it. He was the perfect husband. He wasn't even jealous of the other guys I was with. He even liked to watch. He was a saint that way. He always bought three kinds of liquor in case I didn't like two, but I usually I liked all three. But sometimes I felt like beer. I never asked, "How old are you?" Do you say that to a bird or a bear who is a Millionaire? No. They just are who they are. I was his cheerleader and his nurse. I gave him his medications, double doses even to make him feel better. (*Wipes eyes*), and I was a real wife in every way. Yes, THAT way too. Although once they had to call 911. It was his plastic helper that got stuck. But he was full of hope. I gave him hope. He was planning to grow a mustache and he had no hair! How many can say that? You can talk all you want about me, but how many of you are married to someone who gives you hope? I earned this inheritance, and if his free will was to marry me, to tell me his secrets, to let me play cheerleader, he chose me, then, isn't that the American way? To have choices? To be a Millionaire if you want to be one? Once for my birthday he bought me (sniffles) he bought me (*takes out hanky*) money! (*Looks at crib sheet in purse*) (*sniffling*) If there was a villain he would have slain him for me .... (*Gavel*) (*Pushkin pulls Anna off.*) (*Anna calling after over her shoulder*) And my father hurt me so ...

Push   You should have stopped at the mustache.

Hors   Where did you get that slain bit?

Anna   I read it in a book. Pushkin always tells me to read books.

Hors   What book did you start with? ROBINHOOD?

Anna   It was in my motel drawer this morning. See? The Bible (*Holds up torn page of bible.*)

Interviewer   What happened in there?

Hors   Anna Nicole is accused of – of shoplifting at Loveland. You may quote me on that. BIG FONT FRONT PAGE please.

(*Lights flash*)

Interviewer	Anna, what does it feel like to be a Millieionaire widow?
Anna	(*Looks at paper, reads*) Beauteous and wise and God will wipe the tears from our faces.
Interviewer	(*Camera flashing*) Holy Shit!
Anna	(*Freeze*) (*Anna strikes a pose for the lights. Pulls vial from purse. holds up.*) and I thought ahead. I SAVED HIS SPERM. (*Anima hands Horshel a box of candy and a rose. Syringe stuck in rose. He hands to Anna*).
Hors	Your fans are still with you Dolly.
Anna	(*Takes rose*) Thank you Thank you (*waving*) (*Kissing to audience*) (*Starts to sniff rose. Sees/ pulls out syringe. Faints. Interviewer, Pushkin and Horshel crowd around her.*)
Anima	Big font front page please.

SCENE

(*Pushkin talks to Committee*)

Pushkin	(*To audience*) Dear Committee Members, Other Faculty, Advisors, I know I stood before you not too long ago, but I fear I must ask another reprieve from my deadline. I told you that Miss Smith was unstable and that my thesis on her education would demand flexibility. I thought for a while that the gift of

opening her mind would add favorably to my experimentation theories, but it seems there were unanticipated events. First Miss Smith cut up her own toy dog and gave it to herself pretending it was a gift from someone else. This caused the first hospitalization for she simply would not admit her act of complicity. She denied that she did this in order to get public attention. Going so far as to slit her wrists! You can imagine how I felt, with a one week deadline on this interim report. After release she did follow through on one commitment at least and that was a marriage to one of her elderly fans. Then he died. The fortunate part of her breakdown after court appearance was that I was able to witness her behavior in the ambulance. And fellow academics. It was a magnificent example of refractory adolescence. She thought she was going to a family reunion! And the best evidentiary notation was when she thought the ambulance was a bus taking her home. She looked out the window and thought she saw her father having a cook-out. She thought she saw a family portrait but then said she was the only one missing in the picture! And that there was no plate on the table for her. The ambulance driver called her "Sweetie" and that act of kindness is what apparently added to the delusion and made her sick. Reversal symbiosis. He had to give her oxygen.

SCENE

Split stage. Work table and chairs right. Anna's bed stage left. There are stand up window "bars" separating her bed from center stage space.

(Anima looks inside "bars" but cannot get in.) (Anna on one side of stage, in bed, lying down. Doctor at her bedside)

Doctor	Rest Anna, we'll talk more later.
Anna	I'm tired of talking.
Doctor	Well, think then. Think of the things we said. We were talking about your philosophy of life.
Anna	Life is shit then it kills you, Doc.
Doctor	We were talking of more respect for your own body, Anna.
Anna	I leave my body when they're snapping pictures. I let it stay there without me.
Doctor	So you don't respond to being looked at?
Anna	It doesn't matter. I'm never really seen.
Doctor	*(Exiting)* Rest, dear Anna. Rest.
Anna	*(Dozing off)* Horshel, I think the doctor likes me.

(Anima trying to get men's attention but cannot)

SCENE

(Pushkin and Max seated with table between them. (Anima is trying to feed them papers, but is ignored. Hers fall to the floor each time she tries throughout the scene.)

Push	Well this Martin Luther King thing. I was hesitant at first but it's my chance to show my humanities scholarship.
Hors	It's a winner. What blonde celebrity has ever done this before? Name one.
Push	Jayne Mansfield? I don't know too many blonde actresses. Marilyn Monroe?
Hors	Not even close. They were in girlie movies. Here we can show blondes have smarts.
Push	Not that I want this, but the general public will certainly hail us as feminists. I would not want to be laurelled, of course. This is not about me, this is about Anna.
Hors	Well it's a box office dream any way you cut it.
Push	I have my doubts about the acting burden. Perhaps we could start her off by playing Rosa Parks.
Hors	Who was she?

Push	I'm not a producer, but we could have Anna go to the back of the bus and we could have a Thoreau essay on Civil Disobedience, voice over ... something like that.
Hors	Nah. Anna will want the lead.
Pushkin	*(Anima attempting to feed papers)* I'm not a producer but there were other women in the civil rights movement if it doesn't work out. Stella Brown, Martha Walker, Della Perkins.
Horshel	STOP. No bit parts. You're the consultant but I'm the businessman. I know what the public wants. We could start with a coffin standing up in the middle of the stage and Anna could step out of it like a door.
Push	I'm not a designer but I see pink strobe lights on the door when it opens. No, this is wrong. It needs context not lighting. Maybe a blue strobe though.
Hors	Well then, somebody on the side can tell the story while Anna makes all the moves in a tux or something like when Dustin Hoffman played ... like Tootsie but in reverse.
Push	We are losing the message, Horshel. I'm only in this if the message has my name on it.
Hors	Then it's a damn book! I know. I've worked with your kind before.

Push   The whole concept is WHAT IS TRUTH.

Hors   Let's not lose Anna Nicole in this or I'll find me another scholar.

Push   I'm not sure this is right for the Hippodrome.

Hors   You may be right about that. Let's think Las Vegas. Black History month. When is that? We could bus in churches. How are we gonna get Anna on board?

Push   You're her manager.

Hors   But she trusts you.

Pushkin   I am not sleeping with her so forget that.

Hors   You don't have to. Just tell her this is part of that study you keep barking about.

Push   No.

Hors   Yes.

Push   No.

SCENE

Anna and Push and Hors (Enter Push and Hors. Anna wakes startled) (She starts crying)

Anna — Oh, I thought I was at the airport and I was trying to make reservations and no one would help me but Anima, No one would help me get where I needed to go and I was screaming and I didn't have anything on but a feather boa (*starts shaking, face in hands.*)

Hors — This is ridiculous. Airport agents are well trained to help people. You need to settle down Anna. What's the matter? You're not getting enough ink from the trades? You have to get psycho? The photographers are outside and you are blotto.

Anna — I don't want to see anyone.

Push — Anna, it's time to come out into the shining world to embrace your existence. Horschel has some work for you.

Anna — I'm not doing it. Doc says to think of myself, not your fucking PhD.

Push — This is about yourself. Your name will be in my footnotes.

Anna — I don't know Push. Doc says I need to rest a lot now a long time, that a person who took off

	her clothes all the time is not the real me. The real me is shy, and I think he got it right.
Push	You don't have to take off your clothes for this. Well, I have to check with Horshel, but not all of them I'm almost sure. I don't think Martin Luther King did. It's about cultural coordinates, making a white woman of questionable education play the part of a great brilliant black man.
Anna	I don't know Pushkin. Doc says I need hobbies. Not a career. He says cocaine is not a hobby. He said I could do better.
Push	Better than what?
Anna	He says I take my worth from unworthy people.
Push	I beg your pardon.
Anna	Not you I'm sure, but Doc wants me to take up some pastime and not work all the time. I was thinking of playing the piano.
Push	That is splendid Anna.
Anna	But I hate music. There's always a problem.
Push	Yes … a problem there. What makes you happy Anna? Tell me.

Anna	A big shot of tequila and a snort of coke. Maybe two.
Push	Ah, well I remember that.
Hors	So are we set? You are looking swell Anna. We got the guy from *Celebrity* outside ... We can spring you anytime whenever the doc says. We want to make sure we leak it and get a PR guy that won't let the news out. Get it? We'll only let the general public know. (*Winks*) We got TOYS R US rented for your coming home party, big dolls for you, a big Barbie couch, lots of pink and balloons.

(*Enter doctor*)

Doctor	This is not the kind of conversation we can have here. Visiting time is up, gentlemen.
Hors	It's just business. Don't make it personal. (*Doc escorts them out*) And remember I'm the one who pays your goddamn bill. (*Push and Hors exit*)
Anna	No more talk, Doc. Just hold me in your arms awhile. Can't you take off that starched coat just for a while?
Doctor	We have to keep going back Anna. That's where the hurt is.
Anna	It gives me a headache ...

Doctor	The past is a place. Go through that door Anna.
Anna	When I go through the door I bump my head because I was little then, and the door is too low.
Doctor	I understand. Just close your eyes like we practiced and tell me what you see. Try to think silk. Silk.
Anna	(*Closes eyes*) No. No silk. There is no silk. Everything is still plaid but there is no Anima in it. That's good. Right Doc?
Doctor	I think we're rid of her Anna, finally. You're safe now. There are bars on the window. You set some boundaries. Now we want more boundaries to keep you safe.
Anna	You sure those bars keep Anima out? She can't get me in here? My twin. No more faces in the mirror? No more voices in my ear?
Doctor	I promise. She'll never get in again if you stay away from the booze and the drugs.
Anna	These bars on the window, not just to keep me here?
Doctor	Nope you are safe from her forever if you keep your promise to yourself. Now what other worries ... I know you have a lot.

Anna	You bet I have worries. And disappointments too. I always do. What if the things I look forward to aren't worth looking forward to? Like I might think tonight I'm going to cuddle up under an electric blanket with a glass of hot rum, and then I worry that if it won't really be good as I think it will be, so why should I look forward to it, you know what I mean? It's always like that.
Doctor	Anna, we were talking about your sex life before, and you keep evading it. I'd like you to get to the bottom of something besides a bottle.
Anna	Oh yeah. You were saying why I always gave it away. Well when I was little I remember giving away all my toys so nobody would take them from me and hurt me. Once I heard on TV that if a man rapes you, he steals your soul. That always stuck in my mind. SO I figure if I give it to men I won't have to be raped so I'll save my soul! I care so much about going to heaven. I do!
Doctor	I think I see your logic. So back to your baby, Anna. What became of your baby?
Anna	I never had a baby.
Doctor	Your son.
Anna	You are lying. I never had a son.

Doctor	The son who died. What did you feel?
Anna	I didn't feel anything. I don't feel anything. Can I please have a smoke?
Doctor	Soon Anna. We were talking yesterday about Marie Antoinette.
Anna	I remember. I'm not dumb. They cut her head off. The French Revolution. I remember.
Doctor	But first they took away her son.

(Anna is visibly shaken)

Doctor	They made him go to prison.
Anna	How old?
Doctor	Eight.
Anna	NO.
Doctor	The age your son was.
Anna	No.
Doctor	And he stayed there until he died at age 10.
Anna	He died in prison?
Doctor	They made him sing the French national anthem over and over again and again.

Anna	They tortured him?
Doctor	(*Silence*)(*Beat*) Two years that child was kept in prison. But not yours. Your son died quickly of an illness. Warm and cared for. Suddenly. It was a blessing. He was comfortable, not tortured, he was swimming in love when he went.

(Anna starts rocking back and forth moaning and moaning and keening and moaning louder and louder.) (Doctor holding her hand.)

Anna	Why am I feeling this now?
Doc	Each time has its own light Anna.
Anna	(*Crescendo*) OH NO OH NO OH NO. MY BOY. MY BOY. MY BOY. It's almost like what I feel really happened. It's almost as if it was real.
Doctor	It was real.
Anna	No it's not. It can't be. I can't remember.
Doctor	Just because you can't remember doesn't mean it didn't happen.
Anima	(*Turning away from window bars*) (*to audience*) One of you smartass mortals said the enemy is someone whose story you have not heard. Well I guess that makes me the enemy. You want to know my story? Evil needs no reason. It is its own reason. As for me, I never ever got a chance. I was in the same

womb with my twin, but Anna got all the food and I got eternity. I had to fill it up some kind of way … So I came down to play. The more Anna shows her body, the more I feel the lack of mine. But like some idea comes into you when you're humming a song, I come into Anna's when she is doing wrong. I am her song. As long as she drinks I am in the bottle. As long as she smokes, I am in the weed, and so who wouldn't encourage THAT? She let me exist. Bless her fat buttery double churned heart. You out there judging me, think of this. I didn't have a turkey dinner on Sunday, like you all did, or a street lined with big trees, with leaves in piles of pretty colors on the white sidewalk. Maybe I didn't live like you and you didn't have to hurry from one thing to another, like I do. You never had to think, if Anna does not call me in today "What will happen now?" Maybe you walked down a street with houses – with yellow light falling out from the kitchen on the snow. All I had was a future with its big empty mouth, waiting to gobble me, because Anna had the physical form and I had only the air. How would you like it if no one could see you, or hear you, and since no one has ever met me, worst of all is this – nobody will ever miss me! *(Turns to Anna)* Anna, please tell them about me. At least do that. Tell them who I was. You owe me that. Tell them about me. Tell them who I was. *(Exit)*

(Enter Horshel and Pushkin to Anna's room)

Hors	What's this I hear Anna? You giving up your career? After all your hard work and we're booked for a month of weekends. Why, your life would be nearly perfect Anna.
Anna	I am always nearly perfect? What would make me perfect, Horschel? In your eyes.
Push	We are not angry Anna we are disappointed.
Hors	I'm angry, asshole.
Push	Horshel, there is a more excellent way of dealing with Anna.
Anna	Doc says for me to listen to my heart.
Hors	And what do you hear? Another round of Columbian weed?
Push	Those who are attentive to their professions will prosper, Anna. We have an historical play for you.
Hors	Out Pushkin. I will take care of this. I own Anna. By contract.
Push	(*Exiting*) Fine. I'll be outside if you need to spell any two syllable words Hors.
Hors	OUT!!
Anna	Doc says I'm not crazy, Horshel.

Hors   Oh yeah what does he know? How many times has he dragged you into a toilet to puke?

Anna   Doc says I am just sad.

Hors   Well it must be a fucking virus then, because we are all sad, Anna. You let us down. You've been in bed three months. Time to get out. Your fans want you.

Anna   Doc loves me.

Hors   We all love you Anna. And how is this medicine man any different than your oldest friends?

Anna   He touched the cuff of my sleeve one day and fixed it when it was turned backward. So soft. So sweet. So gentle. No one ever did that.

Hors   Christ, I WILL BUY YOU A WARDROBE OF SLEEVES.

Anna   You know I had a son.

Hors   Let bygones be bygones.

Anna   I neglected him.

Hors   A working woman. What do you expect?

Anna   I let other people keep him.

Hors	Nannies, it's the way Anna. You think you invented babysitters? This is keeping you off stage?
Anna	I was just thinking of myself the whole time. My career.
Hors	Shit.
Anna	Who knows what he felt. What they did to him. Maybe he didn't get any snacks.
Hors	Snacks make you fat. Who wants a fat baby? Come to life Anna.
Anna	Maybe they kept him in a playpen.
Hors	You saw him. You brought him. I remember him wailing backstage. He was with you.
Anna	Backstage! What more do you want from me Hors? I can give you everything but myself. I gave that away a long time ago. I want it back.
Hors	Well you can't get the kid back and you didn't kill it. Pneumonia. It happens.
Anna	Marie Antinette was beheaded.
Hors	Oh yeah? I didn't read about it.
Anna	No, a long time ago. They chopped her head off.

Hors	I got 15 more minutes in here Anna.
Anna	They tore her 8 year old son away and he had to sing to the guards in the prison all night.
Hors	I am calling the Doc to spring you out of here.
Anna	And he died in agony without his mother. I wanted to be famous, Horshel.
Hors	You didn't kill it.
Anna	HIM not IT, Horshel. He was a person. Doc says the word fame means hunger, it comes from Fame. That's another language that means hunger and I think he didn't get any food. I got it all. For what?
Hors	Hell you loved him, everyone knows that.
Anna	I did. I loved him. That is something even a kid would know ... I just guess I loved something else more.
Hors	You seem angry Anna.
Anna	No I AM angry, Horshel.
Pushkin	(*To audience*) Gentlemen of the committee, I know this is highly irregular, but since Miss Smith has been incapacitated for 3 months, I see no solution but to change my course of study. Her thinking is wooly, and when I ask her about wooly thinking to further our

inquiry, she thinks I am talking about real wool and wants me to wrap her up in it to keep her warm! You see my consternation. Therefore, I submit to you what I have recorded thus far, and seek to finalize the theme of celebrityhood. I submit to your guidance, and I humbly beseech you for this one extension. Anna threatens to make a comeback, and I must measure my study with that final conclusion.

SCENE

(Doctor, Horshel and Pushkin talking quietly). (Enter Anna in costume made of leaves, green, Autumn colors, white.)

Hors and Push *(In horror)* Anna!

Anna	Why can't you ever say my name like I'm somebody you like? Aren't you glad to see me?
Doctor	Anna what is this costume? You were supposed to check with me first.
Anna	Your line was busy and you said I could do anything I set my mind to.
Doctor	I didn't say ...
Pushkin	Stop her Horshel. She'll be a disaster on stage.
Hors	Once she's been in the booby hatch, my paper work is null and void.

Anna	Anna Marie Antoinette is free of drugs and I'm going out there to my audience. I'm going to talk to them from the heart.
Doc, Push, Hors	Oh No Anna. Not that!
Anna	It's the 4 stages of woman. I saw it on PBS. Spring, she is hopeful, Summer she is full blossom, Fall, mature, and Winter, she grows old gracefully. Doc says I must learn what it is to be a woman. I had the leaves made special.
Doctor	Not like this Anna.
Hors	We learn by our failures.
Anna	I'm not going to fail, sourpuss. Give your Anna a great big good luck kiss. *(She smooches him)* Move aside guys.

(Drum rolls, cat calls, Anna moves center stage) Hors, Push and Doc off to the side.

Anna	*(Arms up in the air)* I'm back!

(Audience hoots and hollers)

Anna	Oh no no, not that. I'm here to talk about my journey as a woman.

(Audience: Take it off. Oh yeah baby)

Anna Oh no, not THAT woman. The woman who knows my fans want to grow along with me. You see I'm in the summer of my life. (*Shakes her green leaves on her front*). I want to blossom and bear fruit...

(*Audience: "lose the leaves," hollering.*)

Anna No NO, you don't understand. Listen. Listen. I have a story about wanting to be a woman before it is Autumn (*shakes her rear with colored leaves*)

(*Audience starts booing*)

Anna Wait wait, Stop stop. I am Anna Marie now (*she starts to back down*) before there are icicles on my leaves (*shakes headdress*) (*Music makes a down note*) (*she signals music to stop*) I want to flourish with you, my audience. You are my only friends!

(*Audience laughing and hissing*)

Anna (*Very upset*) Stop, Listen listen. I'm clean and sober and why not give me a chance, I tried to be everything you wanted me to be. (*She starts crying.*) (*Sits on the edge of stage*) I had this outfit made for you.

(*Hors and Pushkin come in and pick her up by the arms she shakes them off, standing*)

Anna	*(Rips open her blouse. Confronts audience)* Here. This is what you all want. Here. Two of them. Two with nipples. Doc says they are only mammary glands and other stuff. Here. Take your pictures. Nobody cares about my fucking wish, but I'll give you your fucking wish.

(Push and Hors escort her off to Doc's arms)

Hors	The deeper the sorrow, the higher the joy Anna.
Push	Huh?
Hors	Doc told me that.
Doctor	Anna why didn't you check with me?
Anna	You said to take risks.
Doctor	We had tests to do, systems to put in place, measurements.
Push	Any system you measure is changed by the measurement, Doctor.
Anna	I thought you wanted me to change, Horshel.
Hors	Put a big sign on my back that says KICK THIS ASS.

(Enter Anima with big sign.)

Anna	(*Still crying*) Doc, he helped me so much. I found out why the people on TV just went away, they weren't really there at all. They didn't care about me or even if I watched them. They were just pictures of people. On tape. So I wanted to connect ...
Hors	Well maybe we can do something with you Anna yet – that interviewer who wanted to feature you, all dressed, with your pretty cheekbones photographed.
Anna	(*Wiping eyes, recovering*) Well I don't need my pictures taken anymore. Horshel and I don't want the Hippodrome, and I am not trying out for your skin pictures anyway. I am going to have a baby. A baby of my own. (*Holds her stomach*) With or without my audience.
Push	Ah, proof one can be born anything and become another.
Hors	A baby. When?
Doc	I'd say in about 6 months.
Hors	Who? (*Hors looks at Push. Push looks at Hors.*) (*The 3 men stand around Anna*) You're too fragile for this.
Anna	(*Still weakened*) Doc says I am whole and well. And it's a girl. And I'm going to put bows in her hair. And kiss her. And she will be happy and live and live.

Pushkin   And she will thrive. She will thrive Anna, better put.

Anna   Yes thank you Pushkin. Thrive is a bigger word. She will also be a billionaire, remember.

(All react)

Push   Well now, I did – we did – as you remember that one night – we did have a special moment, Anna.

Anna   Yes it only lasted a moment Pushkin. I remember that much.

Hors   I believe I, myself, am on the short list for father, Anna.

Doctor   *(Puts his arm around her shoulders)* Maybe the future is more important than the past.

Anna   See my tummy is already puffy. See? And my son will come visit me. Doc says that's better than being a celebrity.

Hors   But you were our goddess, Anna.

Push   Right you are Horshel, Zeus gave us mortals a gift. He fashioned a beauty in the shape of this young girl and called her Anna. Her name means "all endowed." Her body was made by the gods of flesh and sound. Athena gave her dexterity and resilience. Aphrodite, goddess of

	love, put a spell of seduction around her head and Hermes put prettiness in her brain but she still wanted to learn the way of the world. *(Sternly)* And this mythological analogy was all my idea, remember, if ever repeated to the press.
Anna	Goodbye. Goodbye Horshel, Pushkin. God Bless you (*To audience*) God Bless all of you too I guess. And (*looking up to Heaven*) *(pause)* God Bless you too, *(uncertainly)* God!
Push	She moves in her own weather.
Hors	She'll wind up in a river.
Doc	Why not hope for the best for her? She's happy for the moment.

(Anna and Doc exit, Horshel running after, Anima follows them across stage, closer and closer to them)

Push	That's exactly the way she is. When the Gods made Anna, they let loose all the lust, greed, betrayal and evil, in the world to follow her around, but they cursed her with Hope.

THE END

Photo Credit: Jack Tarasiuk

About the Author

Grace Cavalieri is Maryland's Tenth Poet Laureate. She writes poetry and plays and is a visual artist. She founded, and still produces, "The Poet and The Poem" for podcast and public radio, a series celebrating 46 years on-air and still thriving. Two hundred of her podcasts were launched to the moon with NASA's Lunar Codex —the first ever podcasts on the moon—landing poetry into "The Ocean of Storms." Grace was married to the late Naval Aviator/Sculptor Kenneth Flynn. They have four daughters, four grandchildren and a great grandson. She is an Academy of American Poets Fellow. Among her many books is a Memoir, *Life Upon The Wicked Stage*.

www.ingramcontent.com/pod-product-compliance
Lightning Source LLC
Chambersburg PA
CBHW042049290426
44110CB00001B/7